Counseling African American Marriages and Families

Edward P. Wimberly

Westminster John Knox Press
Louisville, Kentucky

Book design by Jennifer K. Cox
Cover design by Kevin Darst

First edition
Published by Westminster John Knox Press
Louisville, Kentucky

This book is printed on acid-free paper that meets the
American National Standards Institute Z39.48 standard. ∞

PRINTED IN THE UNITED STATES OF AMERICA
99 00 01 02 03 04 05 06 — 10 9 8 7 6 5 4 3 2

Library of Congress Cataloging-in-Publication Data

Wimberly, Edward P., date.
    Counseling African American marriages and families / Edward P.
Wimberly.
        p.   cm. — (Counseling and pastoral theology)
    Includes bibliographical references and index.
    ISBN 0-664-25656-2 (alk. paper)
    1. Afro-Americans—Pastoral counseling of.   2. Marriage counseling.
3. Family counseling.   I. Title.   II. Series.
BV4468.2.A34.W56   1996
259'.12'08996073—dc21   96-46343

Counseling African American
Marriages
and Families

Counseling and Pastoral Theology

Andrew D. Lester, Series Editor

Contents

Foreword

Edward Wimberly has already established himself as a pastoral theologian with particular expertise in introducing his own culture to pastoral counselors who want to be more effective in working cross-culturally with African Americans. Those of us who are Euro-Americans and unfamiliar with the traditions of African Americans will profit from Wimberly's careful inspection of the cultural context that intensifies stress in the African American family. Living with a double consciousness that results from being both African and American, plus the personal wounds of racial oppression and sexism, are the most obvious. He guides pastoral counselors in helping African Americans live biculturally, meaning to appreciate and participate meaningfully in their African heritage while surviving and thriving as Americans in a dominant culture with different values.

The extended family is a primary value in African American culture. To be effective the pastoral counselor must shift from the individualism of Euro-American tradition and attend to transgenerational relationships, communalism, and connectedness (as the feminist pastoral theologians and psychologists are also telling us) when working with African Americans. The extended family contributes to the problems experienced by African Americans, but connecting creatively with the extended family is also a significant source of healing. Wimberly identifies family systems theory as a helpful tool.

Given that a religious worldview is a constant in the African American heritage, Wimberly introduces us to the spiritual values more unique to this culture. A narrative approach to theology and scripture, with guiding metaphors such as God's rule in establishing salvation history and the significance of living in an eschatological community, is more useful than a propositional approach when helping the African American couple or family examine the spiritual context of their relationships.

In the eschatological community the quality of relationships between believers is central for the fulfillment of God's purposes. The love ethic, therefore, is the cornerstone of marriage and family life, which means that "family members and marital partners are to live in their relationships in such a way that all family members are free to grow into their full possibilities as full participants in God's unfolding drama of salvation and as members of the eschatological community."

Wimberly is particularly concerned to recapture "the communal nature of African American marital and family life" and "the mutuality and androgynous models of our heritage of male and female relationships." He confronts sexism that results from the encroachment of conservative Euro-American religious doctrines about patriarchy and rigid views of male and female roles into the African American community. Wimberly shows how pastoral counselors can use narrative approaches to scripture and theology, plus the love ethic norm for relationships, to analyze and critique patterns in African American marriage and family life, specifically in his chapters dealing with sexual dysfunction, extramarital affairs, abuse and violence. His case studies bring theoretical concepts to life.

The *Counseling and Pastoral Theology* Series

The purpose of this series is to address clinical issues that arise among particular populations currently neglected in the literature on pastoral care and counseling (women in lesbian relationships, African American couples, adolescents under stress, women who are depressed, survivors of sexual abuse, adult adoptees, persons with terminal illness, and couples experiencing infertility). This series is committed to enhancing both the theoretical base and the clinical expertise of pastoral caregivers by providing a pastoral theological paradigm that will inform both assessment and intervention with persons in these specific populations.

Many books on pastoral care and counseling are more carefully informed by the behavioral and social sciences than by classical theological disciplines. Pastoral care and counseling specialists have been criticized for ignoring our theological heritage, challenged to reevaluate our idolization of psychology and to claim our unique perspectives on the human predicament. The discipline of pastoral theology has made significant strides in the last decade. The Society for Pastoral Theology was formed in 1985 and now publishes *The Journal of Pastoral Theology*.

Pastoral theology grows out of data gathered from at least three sources: (1) revelation about the human condition uncovered by the social and behavioral sciences, (2) wisdom from the classical theological disciplines, and (3) insight garnered from reflection on the pastoral ministry event. The development of pastoral theology grows out of the dialogue among these three perspectives, each perspective enabled to ask questions of, challenge, and critique the other perspectives.

Each author is clinically experienced and academically prepared to write about the particular population with which she or he is personally concerned and professionally involved. Each author develops a "constructive pastoral theology," resulting in the theological frame of reference that provides the unique perspective from which a pastoral person approaches both assessment and intervention. This constructive pastoral theology will enable clinically trained pastors and pastoral care specialists (pastoral counselors, chaplains, Clinical Pastoral Education supervisors) to creatively participate in pastoral relationships that effectively enable healing, sustaining, guiding, reconciling, and liberating.

Though the focus will be on offering pastoral care and counseling to individuals, couples, and families, each author is cognizant of the interaction between individuals and their environment. These books will consider the effects of larger systems—from family of origin to cultural constructs. Each author will use case material from her or his clinical pastoral ministry that will serve to focus the reader's attention on the issues faced by the particular population as viewed from the pastoral theological paradigm.

My thanks to colleagues who faithfully served on the Advisory Committee and spent many hours in creative work to ensure that this series would make a substantial contribution: Bonnie Miller-McLemore (1992–96), Nancy Ramsay (1992–96), Han van den Blink (1992–94), Larry Graham (1994–96), Linda Kirkland-Harris (1994–96).

Andrew D. Lester
Brite Divinity School

Acknowledgments

After this book was completed, the Million Man March took place in Washington, D.C. Of note is the turning of the primary focus of African American men from the social forces that have crippled them since slavery to what they themselves can do about their own situation in spite of the tremendous odds. African American men have a renewed interest in family and marital relationships and in the appropriate roles they must play within families.

I find this book timely because of this groundswell of interest in African American family and male and female relationships. Over the years many persons have helped me shape my ideas about marital and family relationships that are reflected in this book. The most significant has been my wife, Anne Streaty Wimberly, whose commitment to marriage and family life in a cross-generational way has been an inspiration to me. Since 1968 Archie and Jerry Smith have been dialogical colleagues who have helped shape my ideas. Tamara Battice, Rita Bigham, and Betsey Ellingsen provided the necessary technical support for this project. My colleagues in the Society for Pastoral Theology have encouraged me to develop my ideas by giving me a forum for expressing them. Andrew Lester and an editorial committee representing Westminster John Knox Press came to me with the idea of writing a book in this area, and I am grateful for their suggestion and support as this book unfolded. I am also indebted to the Status, Tenure, and Welfare Committee of the Interdenominational Theological Center who provided financial resources to undergird this effort.

Chapter One

Beyond
African American Male
Hierarchical Leadership

This book is intended to help practitioners of marriage and family pastoral counseling to be aware of the religious worldview and metaphors that many African American spouses and family members bring to pastoral counseling. Such an awareness will influence the assessment and intervention strategies that might be used when working with these marriages and families. Nancy Boyd-Franklin, Henry Mitchell, and Nicholas Lewter have talked about these religious values and worldviews that often accompany African Americans when they come for individual, marital, and family counseling.[1] This work will explore such religious and spiritual values and their function in the therapeutic relationship.

One major theological phenomenon is emerging that some African Americans bring to marriage and family counseling. It has to do with biblical images of the ideal marriage and family. Following many evangelical and conservative Christian movements, some African Americans come to pastoral counseling emphasizing the traditional male leadership within the home, and this emphasis does not seem to help the family achieve its intended goals. In such marriages and families, spouses are engaged in a power struggle in which the husband seeks to dominate and the wife seeks to be out from under the husband's domination. While it appears to me that there are deeper marital and family dynamics at work in these marriages and families than the religious values that are articulated, the fact is that some marriages and families organize their conflict around religious values.

Given the history of racism and discrimination and some experts talking about the emasculation of African American men, it does seem that male leadership in the home is very important. However, this male leadership is often expressed through utilizing stereotypical images of masculinity and femininity that permeate all of society.[2] Drawing on these stereotypical images, many African American men have sought the sanction of religion to support a particular type of domineering leadership style in the home that is oppressive rather than liberating to the growth potential of their spouses and children. Rigid role definitions are enacted and scripture is drawn on for authority. Such dynamics present real problems for marriage and family therapists.

Often wives also want to be accommodating to the religious values that they feel are important. However, they are in conflict because they feel that what they are expected to do does not lead to their growth and development. Consequently, many are in a spiritual quandary.

Theologically, this use of scripture to support stereotypical and hierarchical roles of males and females within African American marriages and families raises the question about how scripture is being used. Three alternative approaches are possible.[3] The first approach is the *propositional model.* This model emphasizes cognitive uses of scripture that formulate truth into objective realities and call for rational and behavioral allegiance by its adherents. The second approach is the *experiential-expressive model.* This model puts emphasis on the inner feelings, attitudes, and experiences of people. It draws on the experiences of people and makes scripture secondary when understanding family relationships. The third approach is the *cultural linguistic or narrative model.* This model emphasizes the narrative orientation to life and demonstrates how narrative organizes life and informs experience.[4] Rather than seeking sanctions for marital and family relationships in theological propositions or in the experience of marital partners or family members, this approach looks to scripture as narrative to inform marital and family relationships.

The relationship among these three forms of organizing marital and family experience is not necessarily exclusive. They represent divergent aspects of organizing experience and can inform how people in marriage and families utilize religious values. The concern here is that propositional statements are made about male and female relationships and relationships between family members that exclude the experiences of other family members and produce dysfunctional families. Moreover, focusing on individual experiences of family members could lead to making one family member's experience normative for all family members. This too could end up in marital and family dysfunction. However, the narrative approach to utilizing scripture holds out the potential for developing marital and family interactive patterns that allow for each family member to grow and develop.

Scripture is much more dynamic in quality than either propositional or experiential-expressive approaches allow. The narrative model captures better the dynamic way scripture can work in the lives of people. The narrative approach to scripture challenges both the nongrowth-producing propositions that people make and the self-centered use of experience.[5]

Therefore, a narrative approach that understands the function of scripture in interaction with human beings offers an important way to approach marriages and families. It is especially useful with families that have a tendency to make rigid propositions about male and female role relationships. Consequently, narrative theology and narrative approaches to scripture will be utilized to give direction for assessing and intervening with African American marriages and families that have the tendency to develop inflexible role boundaries rooted in propositional understandings.

Narrative approaches to marital and family life are more consistent with how African American families have brought meaning to their lives in the past. Scripture has been very important in the African American church and in African American families, and the method of bringing meaning to the lives of people has been relating their lives to the dominant stories of the Bible. For example, it is not unusual to hear the storytellers of family history tell the family history in relationship to the Christian story especially the exodus story. Consequently, narrative approaches, where people bring meaning to their lives by relating them to biblical stories and plots, have been very important in African American family traditions.

This does not mean, however, that propositional approaches are not necessary. Rather, it emphasizes a more holistic approach that involves both sides of the brain. Propositional or rational uses of scripture alone are not sufficient to inform the marital and family life of many African Americans. Consequently, the narrative perspective permits African American marriages and families to be more flexible with regard to roles and family patterns as they respond to the problems that they confront.

The next section will lay the foundation for utilizing narrative in pastoral counseling with African American marriages and families.

Narrative Theology

Narrative is the telling and retelling of a community's story, the meaning of which unfolds through the interaction of characters over time.[6] A narrative theology focuses on the elucidation, examination, and transformation of the religious convictions that make up the faith of a given community.[7] In the process of reflection on the faith and beliefs of a given community, the narrative theologian attends to the linguistic structures that represent the source and ground of the community's convictions.[8] The narrative theologian not only attends to the propositional level of the belief systems of a faith community, but also keeps the underlying narrative and the events and activities surrounding it in focus.[9] Consequently, narrative theology is an abstraction from the concrete life and interaction of a community of faith.

From the point of view of the Christian faith, *narrative theology* is reflection on the Christian faith story as told and retold in scripture and in the traditions that proclaim Jesus Christ as Savior and Lord. For many Christians this story is about God establishing God's rule in history, and scriptures are viewed as a narrative recording of the events that unfold in God's establishing salvation history.[10] In this historical view of faith, scriptures become the living memory of the faith community to which they return over and over again in the retelling of its story.

For the purposes of this book, the rule of God is the primary metaphor used to understand the unfolding of God's purposes in history. This metaphor is a level of abstraction from the concrete history of the Christian faith community as it is expressed in the Hebrew scriptures and in the New Testament. Therefore, the present canon in scripture is normative, and the traditions utilizing this narrative memory are also sources for interpretation of the church's faith and practice. The term "normative" here refers to the present canon as the major source for understanding God's history of salvation beginning with creation and moving to the eschaton.

The narrative theology articulated here takes very seriously the embodiment of the rule of God in Jesus Christ. The Gospels proclaim Jesus as the incarnation of God who inaugurated the rule of God concretely in history. This was the preaching of the Gospels and the entire early church. This incarnation of God in history did not end with the death of Jesus. It continues today within the church through the power of the Holy Spirit. Theologically, the narrative of God's unfolding purposes and God's establishing God's rule in history continues through the church.

In order for this narrative memory and history to be relevant for marriage and family life, it is necessary to further reflect on the nature of God's rule and reign. Further abstractions are needed on the narrative history of the faith community in order to make a connection between the flow of what H. Richard Niebuhr calls the external history of a community of faith and the internal history of people who live in particular communities.[11] *External history* has to do with the ongoing thrust of God's unfolding history, and *internal history* has to do with how this history impacts the lives of people in community.

Narrative Theology and
Marriage and Family Counseling

The implication of narrative theology for marriage and family life must be explored in relationship to another metaphor. The metaphor eschatological community is closely related to the rule of God. The *eschatological community* is the faith community that exists between the time Jesus inaugurated the rule of God and the time it is finally established at the end of time. This community is made up of the persons who have consciously decided to participate in God's unfolding story of salvation and who have given their lives over to the rule and reign of God. In Niebuhr's terminology, these people have taken the leap of faith; they have moved from observers of God's story to participants in it.[12] In other words, the external history of God has become their inner history.

In the eschatological community, how people live in relationship to one another is essential as God's purposes continue to unfold in its midst. The scriptures emphasize that the quality of relationships among people is extremely significant for the fulfillment of God's purposes. Therefore, communal ethics and the kind of communal atmosphere created are important within the eschatological community.

Abstracting further from the narrative history as recorded in scripture, the ethical norm of love seems to be central, especially to the early church as an eschatological community. This is found particularly in Paul's thinking as he reflects on the significance of the theology of the cross and Jesus' life, death, and resurrection. This same love motif is found in the Gospels and Johannine biblical literature. Jesus' relationships with others were to be imitated and the quality of relationships of support and care was to be primary in the eschatological community. Welcoming strangers to the eschatological community regardless of race or gender was very important in the early church, particularly in the house churches in Rome.[13] Brotherly and sisterly love extended beyond cultural and racial lines. Participation in God's salvation history was viewed as a family affair, and all were invited to be members of this eschatological family without regard to gender, race, or cultural background.

Through the power of the Holy Spirit, the early church saw itself empowered to live a faithful life of love as it patiently awaited the completion of God's rule. This same love ethic and quality of caring in relationship are informative for the eschatological community today. It is possible to draw an analogy between the eschatological community and individual marriages and families that make up the eschatological community, that is, marriages and families also are to live under the love ethic. Marital partners and family members are to live in such a way in their relationships that care and support of others are central. Quality living is essential to the fulfillment of God's purposes even today.

An additional abstraction is necessary to be specific about the love ethic. This specificity has to do with developing a norm from the narrative history of the eschatological community. The norm I have abstracted from the love ethic for guiding marital and family relationships is: *Family members and marital partners are to live in their relationships in such a way that all family members are free to grow into their full possibilities as full participants in God's unfolding drama of salvation and as members of the eschatological community.* This refined norm will serve as the basis of the pastoral theology needed to assess and intervene in African American marriages and families.

From the above principle, it can be visualized that narrative theology also has its propositional elements. Propositional dimensions of thought cannot be eliminated. From my vantage point, propositional statements need to be minimal, and they also need to be stated at the nonnegotiable normative level of abstraction to give guidance to human interaction. Therefore, normative statements need to be made to provide goals toward which African American marriages and families need to move. However, specific roles can only be defined by marital partners and family members as they interact in concrete life situations as they move toward the goals.

Theological Method

In the above information, the beginnings of a theological method are outlined. *Pastoral theological method,* for the purposes here, refers to the level of abstract reflection needed to assist pastoral counselors working with African American marriages and families. This method involves attending to themes, values, and traditions that have nurtured African American families historically: communalism, extended family emphases, egalitarian roles, and a religious orientation. The method also involves establishing abstract norms from the narrative faith history of scripture and the historical values of African American family experience that will serve as the basis for critical analysis of marital and family relationships of African Americans. The norm also needs to be adequate enough to critically analyze the social and cultural forces influencing the lives of African Americans. Finally, this norm needs to serve as a basis on which to draw from the behavioral sciences methods and theories that might help in assessing and intervening in African American marriages and families.

The norm I have chosen has been stated as family members living in ways that liberate the growth potential of each family member. This means that no family member or marital partner lives at the expense of other family members. This norm will be spelled out further focusing on the specifics of what this means in concrete situations. Moreover, it will be the basis on which to interpret scripture and draw from the behavioral sciences.

The specific method of interpreting scripture is called Scripture Interpreting Scripture.[14] This method refers to reading specific parts of the Bible in light of other more definitive aspects of the Bible. Here the emphasis is on the ethic of love abstracted from the experienced narrative of the eschatological community of faith. This norm has been spelled out for its meaning within marital and family relationships. Consequently, this ethical norm of love will help to interpret particular passages of scripture dealing with family and marriage relationships. This method of interpretation seeks to interpret particular passages in their original context and meaning while also using the abstracted norm of love emerging out of the narrative thrust of God's salvation history.

In summary, the overarching theological and ethical norm that informs pastoral counseling with African American marriages and families is the love ethic. This ethic has been refined to involve each family member living in ways that liberate the growth and development of each family member as full participants in God's unfolding drama of salvation. In other words, the emphasis will be on marriages and families as environments for encouraging the holistic growth of marital partners and family members. This norm will be used to interpret scripture and to draw from the behavioral sciences; to evaluate the history of marital and family relationships within the African American community; and to deal with sexism within the African American community. On the basis of this norm and the results of using it, implications for assessing and intervening in African American marriages and families will be drawn.

The significance of the norm of love, expressed through liberating holistic growth dimensions for marriages and families, relates to how marriages and families utilize scripture. The criteria is whether or not scripture is used in ways that promote the holistic liberated growth of each family member. If the propositional use of scripture seems to benefit some family members and not others, then such uses need to be revised.

The second significance of this norm is that it gives guidance to pastoral counselors who work with people who utilize scripture. The pastoral counselor can help counselees to explore whether or not their uses of scripture promote or hinder the liberated holistic growth of each marital partner and family member.

The major concern of this book is to help promote the development of healthy personal, marital, and family stories or mythologies that facilitate the growth and development of each family member. Further, such liberated growth is not envisaged as an end in itself. Rather, the ultimate end of growth facilitation is participation in the unfolding drama of God's salvation. The purpose of the eschatological community is to make people ready to assume their roles and vocations in God's salvation endeavor. Consequently, marital and family relationships serve a greater end.

Pastoral Counseling with African American Marriages and Families

This book is addressed to pastoral counselors and religious counselors who are interested in marriage and family counseling with African Americans. Therefore the uniqueness of African American marriages and families must be identified. Moreover, the distinctiveness of the approach for working with African American marriages and families needs to be identified as well.

The distinctiveness with regard to African American marital and family life can be identified in terms of themes, values, and emphases. For example, the themes, values, and emphases are communal and extended-family-oriented as opposed to individualistic thrusts that are characteristic of wider cultural emphases. This does not make African American marriages and families unique from other marriages and families that are ethnic. However, communal and extended-family values are unique when compared to wider cultural emphases on individualism.

In addition, the communal and extended-family orientations are legitimate for African survival in the Western world. This means that it is very difficult for African American families and marriages to survive without connectedness to extended-family traditions.

A second value is the historical presence of two marital and family life traditions of African Americans. The first tradition is the emphasis on the patriarchal male leadership in marriage and family life that goes back to slavery as a means to reclaim the African American family. The second tradition is a mutuality and androgynous tradition that envisages husbands and wives working together in order to survive oppression and racism. Here again the two traditions are not necessarily distinctive from other traditions in wider culture. Yet the cultural context that gave rise to these traditions is unique, that is, oppression and racism helped to foster responses that eventuated in unique emphases for African American marriages and families.

Patriarchalism is also an African survival form. Its nature is different from Western patriarchalism according to some scholars, for example, I find the work of Charles Finch helpful in this regard.[15] Summarizing his views in an article, I state:

> He illustrates that patriarchy was an inevitable outgrowth of the development of human consciousness related to a number of economic and social factors. He indicates that matriarchy lost ground because it was one-sided, all consuming, and unhealthy in the same way that patriarchy has become today. According to Finch, Africa, particularly Egypt, avoided the split between matriarchy and patriarchy that dominated the rest of the world. He notes that there was a creative reconciliation between matriarchy and patriarchy in lower cultures of the Nile where patriarchy did not overcompensate for the abuses of matriarchy.[16]

Finch points out that matriarchy preceded patriarchy prior to written history and was as abusive as patriarchy is today.[17] His point is that African patriarchy was more androgynous and egalitarian than Western forms of patriarchy.

While African Americans inherited a more mutual form of patriarchalism, we are being influenced to adopt a more deadly form of patriarchalism that is destructive of African American females. That is, African American men are abandoning androgyny and mutuality of African patriarchalism for a model that is destructive to the growth of African American women. Consequently, part of the need is to be more in touch with the mutuality traditions that are part of our African and African American past.

One way to do this is to help African Americans to be *bicultural.* This means that they need to live in two cultures at the same time. They must appropriate the mutuality and androgynous traditions of the African and African American past while living in a culture that has a different focus.

The major themes from the African American past that this book appropriates are (1) the communal nature of African American marital and family life and (2) the mutuality and androgynous models of our heritage of male and female relationships.

In addition to these two themes there are healing traditions of care that make up the heritage of African Americans. The healing tradition consists of a communal support systems approach to marital and family life. This means finding the sources of care for marriages and families from within the extended family.

It is my belief that the healing power of the African American extended family can be enhanced by the modern family systems approaches to marriage and family life. Consequently, cross-generational emphases will be the constant thrust of this book, and family systems theories that feature cross-generational connections will be emphasized.

A valid criticism can be launched that what this book is doing is not much different from what some text books do in marriage and family therapy. While this criticism has some validity, it must be recognized that a cross-generational emphasis is nothing new to African Americans. This has been a consistent theme for us emerging out of our African roots. It is not a new therapeutic trend. Consequently, I draw on contemporary cross-generational theories to assist in helping African American marriages and families continue a distinctive historical thrust.

In my mind, making cross-generational connections is living biculturally, that is to say, connecting cross-generationally puts African Americans in touch with a heritage of mutuality and androgyny that is unique and different from wider culture. Moreover, connectedness to the extended family brings with it resources from the past that are necessary for marital and family survival in contemporary life. Being in touch cross-generationally enables African Americans to live in a culture far different from itself.

I see many African Americans who do not realize the value of extended-family connections. They seem to feel that cutoffs from the extended-family are what is needed to survive in the corporate segments of our economy. However, the opposite is proving to be true. Many African Americans are discovering that connectedness with the cross-generational extended family is not a luxury but an absolute necessity. Therefore, the role of pastoral counseling with African American marriages and families focuses on helping them to recover extended-family connections. Using modern cross-generational methods of therapy are not novel, but they are essential in recovery of a vital African American marriage and family life. What makes this book distinctive is that it seeks to recover a unique and distinctive historical thrust rooted in African and African American communalism and the extended family.

The recovery of the egalitarian and androgynous past is consistent with the narrative theological thrust of this book. These models are very compatible with the growth norm and the ethic of love. This book, however, does not emphasize African patriarchalism. Rather, it lifts up the egalitarian and androgynous traditions of the past that have facilitated growth and love. Therefore, the emphasis is on equality and growth for both marital partners and for each family member.

In summary, the values that inform African American marriages and families are biblical views regarding male and female relationships, affinity for narrative more than propositional approaches to theology, communalism, extended-family orientation, healing tradition of support systems, cross-generational connectedness, and a religious orientation. None of these values represents anything unique to African American marriages and families. However, taken together as a coherent worldview undergirding African American marriages and families, these relationships are unique and distinguishable from orientations in wider culture.

Additional values that are related to the religious orientation will be covered in the next chapter in greater detail.

Chapter Two

Male and Female,
God Created Them
to Be Whole

An African American mother came to counseling initially because she felt she was an inadequate mother. She had just discovered that her seventeen-year-old daughter had been molested when she was eight years old. Her daughter was having difficulty in school and at home. The daughter told her mother that part of the problem was that the mother was inadequate, because the mother had not protected the daughter from the molestation. The mother was devastated, and she felt that the daughter had told the truth. The mother also recalled that she too had not been protected from molestation by a close family member when she was a child. The mother also discovered that the molestation pattern occurred with her own mother. Therefore, she discovered that the pattern of molestation was a multigenerational pattern. For three generations, and perhaps more generations, the female family members were molested by male family members.

The mother came to counseling to help get her relationship with her daughter on a better footing. She also wanted to work on personal issues that could help her come to grips with family of origin issues related to victimization at the hands of male family members. In the process of counseling she confronted a major form of helplessness that was passed on from generation to generation by her mother. This helplessness said that you must remain quiet in the face of sexual molestation, and it was impossible to do anything about it. Early in counseling she learned to confront her mother about her own feelings about molestation. She was also able to allow her daughter to work through her daughter's feelings about her ineptness as a parent. After a year, she was able to confront her daughter's perpetrator and her family that allowed this to happen. She had made up her mind that the cycle of family silence had to stop, because there were other young girls at risk in the extended family.

One of the reasons why this counselee was able to break the silence after several generations relates to her desire to be better connected to her family of origin. Because of the molestation, she felt alienated from her mother and her relatives. She withdrew from them as a protective measure; however, she felt like she was dying inside. Being cut off from her family of origin felt like "soul murder." She did not feel like a whole person as a result. Consequently, she desired to reconnect with her family, and she felt she had to confront the silence about sexual molestation as part of her reconnecting to her family of origin.

The sexual molestation also resulted in her alienation from the church. She had a very deep faith in God. However, because of the history of sexual molestation, she was vulnerable to sexual exploitation. Often, this sexual exploitation came at the hands of church leaders. She withdrew from the church to protect herself from this form of sexual exploitation and to gain more control of her life. The point is that she desired to reconnect with the church, because she felt cut off from another source of her identity. She was a very spiritual person and felt the need for spiritual nurturing through the church.

Throughout my counseling with this mother and her daughter several religious themes were prominent. Among these themes was the need for connectedness to a family tradition and a religious tradition. Pivotal in the themes was the need for wholeness. The need to overcome past abuse, the need to be in charge of one's own physical body and to protect it from abuse from others, the need to have spiritual integrity, and the need for family connectedness are themes of wholeness.

The theme of wholeness and its subthemes are present in the lives of many African Americans with whom I do pastoral counseling. The dominance of these themes relate largely to the presence of a theological worldview that nurtures African Americans' understanding of themselves as whole persons. This theological worldview also helps to distinguish what African Americans bring to pastoral counseling from what non-African Americans bring. My presupposition is that the theological themes and spiritual issues that African Americans bring to pastoral counseling are unique, because the themes and issues are shaped by a unique theological worldview. Therefore, this chapter will explore the themes of this theological worldview and their implications for pastoral counseling with African American marriages and families.

The uniqueness of African American marriages and families is in the theological worldview that undergirds their marriage and family life. The worldview has many religious themes that emerge from the African American religious experience and help to shape how many people behave within African American marriages and families. The themes that dominate this worldview include (1) the embodied soul, (2) the uniqueness of persons, (3) and the family of God. These three themes undergird the values that were identified in chapter 1, namely, communalism, extended-

family orientation, cross-generational connectedness, religious orientation, and living biculturally. This chapter will explore these themes in detail. The goals of this exploration are to (1) identify the theological content
of these themes, (2) identify the biblical and theological traditions undergirding these themes, (3) examine the theological and biblical scholarship
related to these themes that support a narrative orientation rather than a
propositional orientation, (4) draw implications of the examination of these
themes for pastoral counseling with African American marriages and families, and (5) make constructive theological statements about the nature of
persons rooted in extrapolations from the vision of the eschatological community and to balance self-love and other-love.

An Embodied Soul

In 1982 my wife and I took a sabbatical leave from the School of Theology at Claremont in Claremont, California, where we worked with
Howard Clinebell and John Cobb. I remember using the term "soul" on
one occasion with John Cobb. His response to me was that African American theologians were fortunate to be able to use the word "soul." He
pointed out that Western theology abandoned the word, primarily because
of the Greek influence. The concept of the self took the place of the soul.

The concept of the soul remains significant for many African American
theologians. The word "soul" appears prominently in the titles of significant books by such people as James Cone, Henry Mitchell, and Nicholas
Cooper Lewter.[1] Some African American psychologists also use the concept in their book titles. The most notable is *Roots of Soul* by Alfred Pasteur
and Ivory Toldson.[2] Linda Hollies includes the word "souls" in her edited
work by womanist writers, *Womanist Care: How to Tend the Souls of Women*.[3]
Anne Wimberly uses the concept of soul in her work *Soul Stories: African
American Christian Education*.[4]

Of great significance is the fact that the concept of soul within African
American theology largely avoids the ancient Gnostic dualistic split between soul and body or flesh and spirit. Mitchell and Lewter point this out.
They believe that the soul is embodied, because it is both physical and related to its social context.[5]

For Mitchell and Lewter *soul theology* forms a belief system that sustains
and supports African Americans' journey in the United States.[6] This belief
system is made up of core beliefs that enable African Americans to function at full capacity physically, intellectually, emotionally, and spiritually.[7]
Mitchell and Lewter point out that these core beliefs enable African Americans "to affirm their own gender, ethnicity, and peculiar personhood and
still be other-centered and self giving."[8] This belief system fosters a positive

sense of relationship both to God and God's creation and to the family, extended family, and community. The various affirmations have their roots in the Bible that reflect African and biblical wisdom.[9] Oral tradition forms soul theology and passes it on from generation to generation. Mitchell and Lewter call soul theology "doctrine-in-narrative form."[10] About the narrative basis of soul theology Mitchell and Lewter say:

> Soul theology speaks also to the idea of the canon, the corpus of narratives deemed worthy of memory and transmission to succeeding generations. There is little question that the most popular tales in African tradition were told for their usefulness and effectiveness. Likewise, Moses, the emancipator, and Jesus, the suffering Son of God and link to heaven, were themes chosen by African-Americans in the crucible of need.[11]

The embodied nature of the soul is envisaged through defining what I mean by this concept. By *soul* I mean a purposive entity that pushes and pulls the person toward self-transcendence and unity with God, the ultimate source of the soul's activity. This understanding of the soul derives from and is consistent with the black Christian understanding of the soul.[12]

This definition reflects the African past of African Americans where the physical and spiritual worlds were mutually related and influential and were not mutually exclusive as in Platonic dualism or ancient Gnosticism.[13] With no fixed boundaries, the physical and spiritual worlds interpenetrated each other and were in constant feedback. The soul permitted this mutual feedback and was in constant relationship to God. The soul was not confined to the physical world or to the body, but it traveled within both.

The definition of soul that I am lifting up moves toward an understanding of soul closely akin to the biblical understanding of soul relating to the whole person. Biblically, the concept of soul relates to the entire person as a spiritual and physical unity. The soul is not abstracted from the body but related to the entire person.[14]

It has been pointed out that soul has almost been universally rejected except for Carl Jung.[15] This has not been the case, however, for African Americans. Neither the word "self" nor "ego" dominates the African American's definition of personhood. Rather, the word "soul" seems more inclusive of what psychologists today call the self. For African American Christians soul is essential to understanding the worth and dignity of human beings.

Alice Walker believes that the emphasis on soul is essential for creating an environment for home life of African Americans. She comments on the significance of soul and its definition as she reflects on the enmity between African American males and females:

> In a society in which everything seems expendable, what is to be cherished, protected at all costs, defended with one's life? I am inclined to be-

lieve, sadly, that there was a greater appreciation of the value of one's soul among black people in the past than there is in the present; we have become more like our oppressors than many of us can bear to admit. The expression "to have soul," so frequently used by our ancestors to describe a person of stature, used to mean something. To have money, to have power, to have fame, even to have "freedom," is not at all the same. An inevitable daughter of the people who raised and guided me, in whom I perceived the best as well as the worst, I believe wholeheartedly in the necessity of keeping inviolate the one interior space that is given to all. I believe in the soul.[16]

For Walker soul is that part of the person's life that could not be enslaved unless one permits its enslavement. She believes that one has to make a choice to allow one's soul to be contaminated by what surrounds it. Each person has the responsibility to keep his or her soul in proper shape, because it is the center of our character and ability to live with dignity.

From the above statement a general summary can be made about the nature of the soul for many African American Christians. First, the soul is the center of the person's life.[17] It is that part of the person that encounters God and through which God enlivens the entire person. Second, the soul and the body are intricately connected, and the resources of the spiritual world interpenetrate with the material world.[18] In this view the spiritual world and the material world are not enemies; rather they interpenetrate and are mutually influential. This follows the African religious heritage that envisages the world as a union of spiritual and material. Third, the body and the soul are interrelated.[19] Fourth, the soul not only has a relationship with the body, it also has a relationship with communities. The soul is what enables the person to become a full participant in the life of the community even when that community is continually oppressed. God's empowerment of the soul and spirit in community provides the person the ability to transcend and live in spite of oppression. Fifth, the person is a whole being, and this includes a soul, a body, and relationships with others. In other words, undergirding the personality is a soul that is relational in nature. Finally, the soul is the center that gives meaning to life and helps to shape the core beliefs that sustain lives.

The key constructive statement growing out of this discussion of the soul is that the soul is embodied. It is not isolated from its relational and social context. The view of the embodied soul presented here does not lend itself to individualism that seeks to take human beings out of their relational and social contexts.

The view of the *embodied soul* as relational and participatory in historical events is harmoniously consistent with the liberated growth of persons and the ethic of love growing out of the eschatological community. The concern for the growth of each family member and the concern for one's own growth is related to the embodied soul. The whole person is an embodied soul. The person grows and develops within relationships with others and within particular social contexts. These relationships also include relationships with others across generations. It is impossible for the embodied soul to live in isolation, even though its fundamental orientation begins with the relationship with God. Placing the embodied soul in its relational and social context is essential to its very nature. In short, soul is embodied in physical and social contexts; being relational the soul seeks growth in relationship to God, self, and others.

With regard to the implication for pastoral counseling with African Americans, it needs to be emphasized that connections are important. These connections include family, extended family, and church. Therapists need to keep these connections continuously in mind and use them as therapeutic resources when possible.

The Uniqueness of Persons

Mitchell and Lewter point out that the soul appears before God and receives its unique character.[20] Of great significance is the belief that one is not defined externally nor does one receive his or her uniqueness externally. Uniqueness is a gift of God bestowed by God through God's relationship to persons. In the process of being known by God one receives one's uniqueness.

African Americans believe that the source of one's uniqueness is that they are made in the image of God. They take very seriously the biblical support for this notion that is found in Genesis. The doctrine of the uniqueness of persons generally begins with Genesis 1:26–28. We were created in God's own image and likeness. What does this mean?

First, Adam refers to all humanity. All human beings are God's creation and created in God's own image, both males and females. Second, image and likeness are not separated according to maleness and femaleness in this first creation story. Both males and females share godlikeness. *Godlikeness* also refers to resemblance, representation, similar form—a replica. Likeness and image therefore have to do with the godlikeness that exists in all human beings that are part of creation.[21]

This understanding of likeness and image, I believe, is the source of Alice Walker's notion of soul. It is that dimension of each person that is given by God as part of the created order. This concept also identifies our capacity to transcend the purely animal level or instinctual level. It makes possible our living as God's representatives on earth with the task of assisting God in ruling.

Godlikeness is, indeed, the source of the African American's concept of soul. However, the second creation story in Genesis 2 raises a significant question for African American marriages and families. The issue raised is whether women are derivative of males, and therefore, subject to male leadership. A propositional view of marriage often has drawn on the second creation story interpreted to say that men are viewed as leaders over women. Consequently, this creation story could present some difficulties for African American women and men who want an egalitarian marriage and family. A fresh examination of this passage is important. The work of Phyllis Trible will be explored to bring a different perspective on this issue.

In her book *God and the Rhetoric of Sexuality*, Trible points to some of the common and popular notions about woman being formed from man and being man's helpmate. She makes the following list of popular ideas:

> A male God creates first man (2:7) and last woman (2:22); first means superior and last means inferior or subordinate.
>
> Woman is created for the sake of man: a helpmate to cure his loneliness (2:21–22).
>
> Contrary to nature, woman comes out of man; she is denied even her natural function of birthing and that function is given to man (2:21–22).
>
> Woman is the rib of man, dependent upon him for life.
>
> Taken out of man, woman has a derivative, not an autonomous, existence.
>
> Man names woman and thus has power over her.[22]

Trible points out that these traditional notions supporting male superiority and female inferiority are not accurate and are not present in the story itself. She says that these ideas do not respect the true meaning of the text when one looks at the grammar, themes, and images from the point of view of the overall purpose of the story.

Trible points out, and I agree, that the story is divided into three scenes. The first scene is God's creation of the earth and human beings; the second scene is the disobedience of human beings; and the third scene is the disintegration of God's handiwork. The story conveys the destruction of a harmonious whole created by God. Thus, the story is not about the subjugation of females to males, but the nature of human tragedy. The plot is about how God's original intention for human beings and for the world was disrupted. The original intent was for men and women to live in harmony with each other, with the earth and all earth creatures as well as with God. The Fall, however, introduced the tragic element of sin into human existence.

The third concern of this second story is the damage that came to human beings as a result of the Fall, that is, God laid a curse on human beings and the order of creation because of human disobedience. Remember that God had created human beings to live in harmony with each other. Both males and females were created equal in the image and likeness of God. Gender was part of the created order, but in neither story was there any presupposition of superiority or inferiority. The fact that Adam was nonsexual in both stories is crucial. Moreover, Eve's being created from Adam's rib does not mean that Adam was male. It only points to the fact that Adam was an earth creature and that to become reproductive Adam, or human nature, had to be divided into sexes.

In the Fall the inequality between men and women was created. The hostility and enmity between male and female came into existence. The animosity is the result of the curse, and is not the way it was intended to be. Trible comments on the nature of the relationship between males and females after the Fall.

> Alas, however, union is no more; one flesh is split. The man will not reciprocate the woman's desire; instead, he will rule over her. Thus she lives in unresolved tension. Where once there was mutuality, now there is a hierarchy of division. The man dominates the woman to pervert sexuality. Hence, the woman is corrupted in becoming a slave and the man is corrupted in becoming a master. His supremacy is neither a divine right nor a male prerogative. Her subordination is neither a divine decree nor the female destiny. Both their positions result from shared disobedience. God describes this consequence but does not prescribe it as punishment.[23]

The story ends with Adam and Eve being thrust from the Garden of Eden. Their mutuality is gone. The ground for a life of animosity was established permanently.

Biblically, the key for African American marriages and families is that stereotypical and hierarchical images of males and females are not part of the structure of essential reality. Rather, they are the result of human limitations and frailty. Therefore, the emphasis theologically needs to be on what is possible for males and females in terms of mutuality and sharing. Settling for the stereotypical and hierarchical images of males and females is to limit human possibilities.

Trible's work also helps to envisage the stories in Genesis as narratives rather than as propositions for the relationships. This means that marriage and family life unfolds like narratives, and it is hard to script marital and family life according to rational propositions. Marriage and family life is dynamic, and biblical narrative helps to inform the interactions taking place in marriage and family life.

With regard to marital and family therapy with African Americans, the significance of Trible's interpretation is that therapists need to help counselees envisage possibilities beyond hierarchy. Moreover, the pastoral counselor needs to help African American couples and families to see that there are different traditions of interpretations of Genesis 1—3.

This discussion of Genesis 1—3 needs to be summarized and related to the norm of liberated holistic growth and the ethic of love. The basic question governing this summary is, How does the discussion of these biblical passages help us to expand our understanding of the norm of growth and the ethic of love?

First, both males and females are created in the image of God. Women are not derivatives of men. Thus, males and females share a common humanity and, therefore, they share similar growth needs.

Second, there is no basis at all for making male experience normative for everyone. Rather, males and females have experiences that are gender specific as well as experiences that are common. Particular gender differences, though hard to define, ought not be placed in any hierarchical order or valued more than the other. Experiences of both females and males should be valued and form a complementary interaction to enrich the life of those in the eschatological community.

Finally, gender-linked roles are *not* ontologically established. Rather, they are established socially and should function to make the life of the community better for all who participate. Women attending to the needs of others without thought of developing their own selves, for example, is not consistent with the norm of liberated holistic growth. Moreover, men attending to their own needs without thought of the needs of others is inconsistent with the ethic of love and the norm of liberated holistic growth. Roles exist to serve the needs of individuals and the needs of the community. People are not created to serve the roles.

New Testament Views on Hierarchy

It is not enough to focus on perspectives on Genesis as a way to inform working with African American marriages and families. New Testament perspectives on male and female relationships need to be examined as well.

Robert Jewett, a scholar on Pauline writings, in a chapter entitled "The Sexual Liberation of Paul and His Churches," says that Paul believes that sexual differences were overcome in Christ.[24] Jewett goes on to describe a progression in Paul's thinking from a patriarchal or male-dominating model toward a more egalitarian model of male and female relationships. This can be seen in 1 Corinthians 7:7 where Paul outlines an egalitarian model of male and female relationships. Jewett points out that the Corinthian churches took equality of males and females being copartners in ministry seriously. He identifies androgynous impulses such as women taking on male hairstyles as a sign of their equality. Corinthians viewed males and females as equal and both subject to God.

Jewett points out that Paul's views were altered by later writers from the Pauline school in terms of moderate subjection and later repression of women as reflected in the pastoral epistles. Elisabeth Schüssler Fiorenza supports this by pointing out that Paul leaves the door open for his successors to reinstate the patriarchal relationships.[25] Commenting on Galatians 3:28, she indicates that Paul unequivocally affirmed the equality and charismatic gifts of males and females. She points out that he affirmed women in their leadership roles in the church, their call to a marriage-free life, as well as equal rights for males and females within sexual relationships in marriage. However, Paul left the door open to later reintroduction of patriarchalism, in Fiorenza's mind, when he valued the nonmarried state higher than the married state with regard to missionary work. She feels this restricts the active participation of Christian wives within the Christian community. She concludes that Paul's impact on women is double-edged, emphasizing Christian equality and freedom of women, but subordinating women's behavior in marriage and participation in the church.

The Gospels are clear that the historical Jesus also challenged the male and female stereotypes by the way he related to women. Jesus came announcing that a new order of reality was emerging. This order was different from the reality that existed. The consequences of the Fall had been overcome, and the original creation of males and females in God's own image was restored.

The use of Trible, Jewett, and Fiorenza does not exhaust the scholarship on the various biblical texts that have been discussed. However, the concern here is to attend to those scholars whose hermeneutical interpretations of selected biblical texts are closely associated with narrative models of interpretation, the norm of liberated holistic growth, and the ethic of love. These scholars find traditions within the canon of scripture that transcend the patriarchal model. Within scripture exist egalitarian and mutuality traditions where men and women participate equally in partnership within the household of God.

The point of this discussion for pastoral counseling with African American marriages and families is that scripture moves beyond stereotypical roles of males and females in selected traditions. Consequently, it is possible to help couples and families to move toward a functional understanding of roles in terms of their utility functions for the sake of the marriage or family rather than for the sake of the role itself.

The traditions of scripture emphasized here are consistent with the norm of liberation and the love ethic. The interpretations reviewed here help to free the growth possibilities of each marital partner and family members.

The Family of God and Humanity

Mitchell and Lewter point out that another core soul belief is the affirmation that African Americans are part of the family of God.[26] The sources for this affirmation have biblical bases. The biblical bases for understanding persons as members of the household of God are numerous.[27]

The foundation for the doctrine of the family of God is rooted in the theological metaphor of household. Ephesians 2:19–22 is one scripture that lifts up the household imagery:

> So then you are no longer strangers and sojourners, but you are fellow citizens with the saints and members of the household of God, built upon the foundation of the apostles and prophets, Christ Jesus himself being the cornerstone, in whom the whole structure is joined together and grows into a holy temple in the Lord; in whom you also are built into it for a dwelling place of God in the Spirit.

The metaphor of *household* was used by the writer of Ephesians to describe the inclusion of certain people within the family of God who did not previously belong to this family by tradition. In Jesus Christ the partition that separated persons was broken down (Eph. 2:14) and he declared that strangers are part of the family. Since the time of the writing of Ephesians, many Christians across the centuries have drawn on this image of the household of God to support their own inclusion and participation in the family of God. This is true also for African American Christians.

Deotis Roberts, in *Liberation and Reconciliation: A Black Theology*, addresses this very issue of how the black church drew on Ephesians 3:14–15 and Galatians 6:10 for their inclusion in God's family.

> It is the image of the family which best describes our peoplehood, that offers, I believe, the most constructive possibilities for a theological understanding of the church in general and the black church in particular. Paul, speaking to the church at Ephesus, says: "For this reason I bow my knees before the Father, from whom every family in heaven and on earth is named" (Eph. 3:14–15). Elsewhere he says: "So then, as we have opportunity, let us do good to all men, and especially to those who are of the household of faith" (Gal. 6:10). These words of Paul seem to be written especially for a homeless, hopeless, powerful people.[28]

African American Christians have understood themselves to be included in God's household. Such a sense of belonging has empowered African American Christians' belief that they have worth because God invited them to be participants in the ultimate family, the household of God.

In God's household there is room for all.[29] Members of the household feel not only a kinship toward one another but also a responsibility toward one another. Such a household is patterned after the caregiver Jesus, who is the head of the household of God. One does not receive membership in the household based on one's own effort, but only through the initiative of God. Membership is a gift that cannot be earned; it is bestowed.

Being members of the household of God also brought with it the gift of seeing others within the household as brothers and sisters under the parentage of God (Matt. 12:50; 25:40; Mark 3:31–35; 1 Cor. 1:10–17; 2 Cor. 13:11–12; 1 Tim. 5:1–2).[30] Roberts points to the fact that membership in the household of God transcends the limits of blood relationship.[31] Membership in the household of God, the bestowing of self-acceptance, and the brotherhood and sisterhood of all under the parentage of God are gifts of God that are to lead toward ministry. These gifts are free, but the intent of bestowing them is for those who receive the invitation to enter into God's salvation drama. Roberts, with this understanding, emphasizes that the household of God is a messianic and christological community.[32] Those who accept the invitation become disciples who are to reproduce the activity of God. Those who are invited are to produce fruit and good works. As family members, they become joint workers (1 Cor. 3:9; 2 Cor. 6:1–10). They are fellow servants seeking to do the work leading to God's reign.

African Americans envisioning themselves as members of the household of God has foundation within the New Testament, particularly in Pauline theology. In his article entitled "Tenement Churches and Pauline Love Feasts," Robert Jewett makes the following conclusions: (1) there were inner-city, lower-class tenement churches in addition to more middle-class house churches in the early church; (2) these churches were not governed by an hierarchical model of leadership, but by a form of egalitarian leadership; (3) the attenders at the tenement houses were slaves, ex-slaves, and laborers in a variety of trades; (4) the structure of the tenements was that of high-rise slum dwellings; and (5) many had immigrant status.[33] Commenting on these tenement churches and their communal life, Jewett says:

> They fused sacramental life with regular sharing of material resources in the context of celebrative meals; they joined ecstatic joy at the presence of a new age by forming new families of brothers and sisters to cope with the poverty and alienation in the slums of the inner cities; they united care for the poor with worshipful celebration of Christ as the Lord of the Banquet.[34]

The point is that the egalitarian and sharing traditions of the scripture attracted African American Christians. Just as the early church attracted the poor and oppressed, the scriptures also drew African Americans and helped to meet the religious and spiritual needs of African Americans. Consequently, African Americans saw themselves as part of God's eschatological community where participation was not based on hierarchy, race, or class.

The significance of the doctrine of the household of God for African Americans is manifold. First, membership in God's household confirms that African Americans have worth and value as human beings and as children of God. Second, it supports the idea of extended-family relatedness beyond bloodlines. Third, membership in the household helps to affirm that individuals are not alone and isolated. Fourth, membership also means that individual souls are connected to other souls; these connected souls need to be participants in God's salvation drama. In short, membership within the household of God affirms the worth of each individual soul and helps each individual soul to see himself or herself in relationship with others who participate in a common mission.

The implication of belonging to the household of God for pastoral counseling with African American marriages and families is that pastoral counselors need to call marital partners' and family members' attention to their connectedness to God's household. My wife and I lead many marital enrichment groups with African Americans. We have found that couples with functional or dysfunctional marriages often find their connections with other couples to be very comforting for them. They realize that they are not alone in their struggle and they can find resources from others for their marital journey.

One of the limitations of marital and family counseling is that it does not often involve other couples having similar problems. Finding models where there can be multiple couples and families in pastoral counseling is very important.

Toward a Doctrine of Human Beings

This chapter has explored several key themes undergirding the life of African American marriage and family life. The conclusions of this exploration for a constructive statement about the nature of persons are important. On the basis of this constructive anthropology implications for pastoral counseling with African American marriages and families can be drawn.

1. The soul in the African American Christian experience is a way to talk about the whole person related significantly to God, to the self, to others, and to the community. Therefore, the soul is relational and contextual. The concept of the embodied soul embraces this contextual and relational understanding.

2. The embodied soul participates in a variety of relationships and shares godlikeness. This godlikeness is bestowed on females and males

alike without distinction. Because of this equality of bestowal, male experience is not normative for females. There are experiences that females and males share in common, but there are also experiences that are unique to females and to males.

3. The soul and the godlikeness of males and females grow and develop best in egalitarian and mutual sharing contexts. In these contexts each adult family member and marital partner takes full responsibility for himself or herself as well as creating an environment where all can grow into their full images of God.

4. Achieving liberated growth and the ethic of love within marriage and families is linked to the presence of God in human relationships bringing life, wholeness, and healing within community. Growth occurs best when marriages and families envisage themselves as members of the eschatological community because of the many spiritual and communal resources that are present for nurturing and care.

The implications of these four conclusions for pastoral counseling with African American marriages and families is that the uniqueness of each person and each person's participation in the marriage and family is essential. Helping marriages and families balance self-focus with other-focus is very crucial. The counselor needs to embrace each person as a relational whole who lives and interacts with others in interdependent ways. This means that pastoral counselors need to take the context in which people live and grow very seriously and help marriages and families to create caring environments. Pastoral counselors must take seriously the religious needs of each person recognizing that spirituality places a vital role in human development.

Pastoral counselors also need to challenge marriages and families where marital partners and family members live at the expense of others within the marriage and family. This includes propositional notions that seek to make one person's growth more significant than another's growth. Moreover, the biblical traditions that support egalitarian relationships can be discussed in the counseling session.

This chapter began with a case study of multigenerational abuse that was exposed because a mother refused to be silent any longer. The forces pushing her to confront the abuse openly related to a theological worldview that is at work in her life. This worldview embodies many of the themes that are explored in this chapter. Having themes in mind when doing pastoral counseling with African Americans can assist greatly the therapeutic process.

Chapter Three

The Context
of African American Families

Part of the pastoral theological method involves the analysis of the social forces that impact the marriages and families of African Americans. The purpose of this chapter is to place African American marriages and families in their broadest possible social and cultural context in order to understand the social and cultural influences shaping them.[1] The specific focus is on those factors in society that inform the worldview and metaphors brought to pastoral counseling by African Americans. More precisely, the social forces that inform the worldview undergirding African American marriages and families include (1) bicultural challenges or the pressures involved in living in two cultures at the same time, (2) racial oppression of African American men and women, and (3) religious values governing family and marital relationships.

It is not enough to understand the many social factors informing the worldview that African Americans bring to marriage and family pastoral counseling. It is also important to evaluate the worldview in light of established theological and ethical principles. Therefore, this chapter will seek to evaluate the worldview using the criteria of holistic growth and the ethic of love.

Prior to turning to the context of African American marriages and families, a case study will be presented that illustrates how the social forces, vertical and horizontal stressors, influence marital and family functioning.

The Case of Mr. and Mrs. P

The following couple was referred to me by a local minister. The husband made the contact and pursued me until he finally got an appointment. He indicated that he wanted more emotional intimacy with his wife. She indicated that she came to counseling only for the personal goal of getting her life together. She felt like she eventually wanted a divorce.

Mr. P is forty-five years old and a regional sales manager for a retail company. He likes his job a lot. He says he is successful and makes a decent living. He is in good health. However, he suffers from impotency which he feels has been caused by family and work stress. He dresses very neatly and takes pride in his appearance. He presents himself very well and is articulate.

Mrs. P is thirty-seven years old. She works part-time in a local industrial plant. She gave up a full-time job to move with her husband to his new job. She is very unhappy about the move and would like to return home to be with her extended family. She is on the light heavy side and has a pleasant appearance. She is articulate and communicates her anger facilely.

They have two boys ages three and twelve. They indicate that there is no spillover of their problem with the children. They seem to work very responsibly as parents and cooperate with each other.

Mr. P has been married previously. He has one child from that relationship. The previous marriage does not seem to be a problem in this current relationship.

His goals are marital in nature and her goals are to increase her autonomy and eventually get a divorce. They have been married for fifteen years. Mrs. P complains that she has no life of her own. She feels she has given up too much of her own life to be married. Her expectation was that she would be in the traditional role of a wife and allow her husband to be the head of the house. She expected him to make the decisions and provide for all the family needs.

She is angry with him because he has broken all the promises related to him as a provider. They have severe financial difficulties, including credit card problems. They have had plenty of money, but their spending has outstripped their means. He insists that the problems were not his fault. He also believes that he found himself in circumstances beyond his control.

They interact in a very argumentative way. He tries to explain and defend his behavior to her, dominates the conversation, and interrupts his wife. She will listen quietly until there is an opening. Then, she will enter the conversation. Sometimes she makes blaming accusations.

He is motivated to come to counseling because he is convinced she wants out of the marriage. This causes him great anxiety and he attempts to exert more control over her life to keep her from leaving.

The family history of the couple is also important. Mr. P has four brothers and sisters, of which he is the oldest. His mother and father liked to brag about his intellectual gifts. However, his mother was disabled permanently from a serious illness, and it was his job to care for his younger brothers and sisters.

He described his early family life as a child and an adolescent as one of continuous moving from place to place. There were financial problems, and it seemed as if they moved every time the rent was due. His father was a laborer, and his mother was unable to work. He said he attended at least five or six different schools as a child.

In this context of poverty, he promised himself that he would never be as poor as his parents were. He made a vow that he would not approach life in the same manner his father approached life and accepted poverty. He despised the way his father lived and was determined to be a better provider than his father.

Mrs. P also was responsible for her younger brothers and sisters. She was the oldest and she felt as if she lost her childhood. She said that her mother abdicated her parental role. Mrs. P felt as if her mother manipulated her to become the mother so that she could be free from parental responsibility. She felt like she was the free baby-sitter. She also said that her mother never appreciated what she did and that she never had anything good to say about her.

In summary, both Mr. and Mrs. P brought to their marriage poor relationships with their families of origin. They both had resentments related to being forced to be caretakers of their younger brothers and sisters. They learned adult roles prematurely and did not have happy childhoods.

With this case material in mind, it is time to turn to the social factors that were influencing their relationship.

Bicultural Concerns

Mr. P grew up in a very poor family and promised himself that he would never be as poor as his family of origin. His poverty created in him a desire to have high economic class status and to be materially successful. Mrs. P grew up in a family that had adequate resources, and she was happy with fewer things materially. They often argued about his need to have more and more things and constantly going into debt as a result. She felt she would have been happier renting a house or an apartment, rather than having a large house note and a car payment.

Both Mr. and Mrs. P felt that they needed to have contact with the African American community. They wanted to be rooted socially in the black community, and they did this through participation in an African American church. They held this desire in common, and this was what kept them together: they both were very involved in their church.

Mr. and Mrs. P were bicultural people. Bicultural refers to a theoretical concept that first appeared in the writings of W.E.B. Du Bois which he called double consciousness.[2] Bicultural relates to a sense of twoness, or being both African and American at the same time.

Andrew Billingsley has explored this concept of double consciousness recently.[3] He discovered that many parents taught their children to be both black and American simultaneously. Part of this education was being related to the African heritage, which included dress, language, family customs, and the inherited worldview of being related to extended family. Of critical importance in double consciousness is having the proper balance between the African American heritage and assimilation into American culture. Total assimilation is considered cultural suicide, while total immersion in African American culture is considered unwise.

Part of the social forces giving shape to the worldview of Mr. and Mrs. P were marketplace values and achieving corporate success. On the one hand, he was unbalanced in his commitment to being American. His wife, on the other hand, seemed to want more of a balance.

As Mr. P attempted to overcome his background of poverty and outdo his father, he found himself trapped in the marketplace, which produced a great deal of stress for him and his family. He was constantly on the road. He had very little quality time with his wife or his children. He was never relaxed at home. He seemed to be constantly preoccupied with what was going on at work. He felt extremely vulnerable at work because he was not sure how he was doing. He felt overly scrutinized by his supervisor, and worried about being fired. Consequently, he expected his wife to make up for the inadequacies he felt on the job. He wanted her to be there for him at all times. He expected his life and job to be the center of their lives. He began to blame her for his shortcomings and inability to be what he wanted to be as a corporate-type executive.

In the past, real success in the marketplace came as the result of seeing the proper relationship between the cultural heritage and the workplace. Billingsley has pointed out that full assimilation into the marketplace is not the strength of African American families. Building strong institutions, organizations, and alliances based on traditional values, and cultural history and heritage have been the key to the success of African Americans in the marketplace.[4] The source of full participation in wider society comes from being related significantly to the African American cultural heritage. Being alienated from this cultural heritage makes marriages and families vulnerable to marital dysfunction.

Fortunately, Mr. and Mrs. P were forging the cultural link through the church. This held out the potential for bringing a better balance between culture and the marketplace. However, the pressure Mr. P was putting on his wife to be his total support at the expense of herself was misplaced and unfair. He needed to realize that the source of his desire to be successful came from deficits in his family of origin, particularly family poverty.

As a pastoral counselor doing marriage and family counseling with Mr. and Mrs. P, I knew it was important to evaluate their bicultural state. However, the proper balance between the cultural heritage and the marketplace could only be determined by the pastoral counselor based on theological and ethical criteria. The question was, To what extent is the balance between cultural heritage and the marketplace liberating for each family member? The answer was that the balance for Mr. P was inadequate. He wanted to live and participate in the marketplace at the expense of his spouse and family. He placed unrealistic demands on them to be there for him. In reality the only real support for the marketplace would be to correct the balance in the direction of increased participation in the cultural heritage. Everyone else in the family had to sacrifice their needs for him.

Therapeutically, several options could be taken. One was to help Mr. P create a better balance between his cultural heritage and the marketplace. Another was to work through his family of origin concerns that made him want to be so successful. Another option was to help him visualize the impact his demands were having on his family. An additional concern was to help him be more responsive to the needs of his family and modify his demands. I worked with both Mr. and Mrs. P, attending to each person's feelings and way of looking at reality, as a means to help them connect at an emotional level. The goal was to create a climate to address the problem of bicultural imbalance.

The key issue in biculturalism is to be aware of the impact that dual participation has on African American families. The impact is real, and a bicultural analysis is essential when working with African American marriages and families.

Racial Discrimination

It was obvious that racial discrimination was another factor shaping the worldview that Mr. and Mrs. P brought to pastoral counseling. Mrs. P did not feel this discrimination because her supervisors were African American. Mr. P, however, felt that he was under constant review by his superiors because of his skin color. It was very difficult to distinguish how his own personal problems helped to muddy the problems he felt at work or whether there was actual discrimination. Yet it is very important to take his worldview seriously as a way to address the concerns raised by both Mr. and Mrs. P. In this section the emphasis is on racial discrimination as a stress factor impacting African American marriages and families.

Racism refers to the combination of the power to dominate by one race over other races or ethnic groups that is grounded in the historical assumption and prejudice that a particular race is innately superior to others.[5] Those who adhere to a conflict theory of human relations make racism totally determinative of everything in the lives of African Americans. However, others like Billingsley focus on how African American families have managed and thrived despite racism. Those who have made racism determinative have analyzed the impact of it on the lives of African Americans. Their conclusions are as follows:

> It is asserted in the literature that black male socialization is developed around three interrelated postulates: (1) that the black male has been emasculated (literally and figuratively) by white society; (2) that the emasculation process has prevented his coming to full maturity; and (3) as a result the black male tends to be a poor husband and father.[6]

Mr. P subscribed to a conflict understanding of his life and work. He believed that he was fatalistically doomed in corporate America. Consequently, he was frantically looking over his shoulder waiting for the white man's hang noose to be slipped over his head. He was constantly stressed and fearful of being discriminated against.

Mrs. P said she used to believe that it was pure racism that Mr. P faced on his job. She, therefore, tried to be emotionally supportive of him. However, she said she began to realize that Mr. P also did things on the job that would aid and abet the racial discrimination. She pointed out that he would always over-spend his expense accounts and did not provide the appropriate documentation. She began to realize that this was a pattern that he repeated over and over again after he had been warned. She indicated she became frustrated when she saw this happen after he changed jobs. When she pointed this out to Mr. P, he accused her of being nonsupportive.

Mrs. P seemed to be better adjusted on her job. She also realized that she needed to give more attention to her own career and leave Mr. P to fend for himself. She felt she had done all she could for him, and he needed to do something for himself. Mr. P was angry about her attitude, and he felt she was emotionally abandoning him. He began to engage in trying to change her mind rather than look at his own contribution to his self-destruction.

Mrs. P seemed to have a different attitude toward racial discrimination from Mr. P. She indicated that she knew it was real. However, she felt it was how one responded to it that made the difference. She believed that she had a choice of whether to internalize the racism and let it harm her. She felt it was possible to make the best of a situation because it was hard to change what was real.

Some reading this account of Mr. and Mrs. P might raise the question concerning Mrs. P's attitude toward her husband. Perhaps the thought comes to mind that she might be a person who is angry with black men regardless of what they do or do not do. This subject did come up. She indicated that she was deeply disappointed in him. She also went on to say that she believed she might be too harsh with him. However, she felt that she had sacrificed too much of herself trying to boost his ego and that his pattern was too well established.

It is important to pursue the idea that Mrs. P's anger toward her husband might be related to internalized racism. Her disappointments could be related to the fact that she might have internalized attitudes toward her husband that were part of the stereotypes held toward black men in wider society. Perhaps the men in her life all disappointed her prior to her marriage. Perhaps her expectations were due to the expectation that she saw her husband as a major protector and provider growing out of the traditional patriarchal expectations of African American husbands and fathers. All these possibilities are plausible, but the last possibility needs some exploration.

Some writers have pointed out that the rules governing African American male and female roles have not changed, even in the 1990s. Renita Weems, in *I Ask for Intimacy*, says that social upheaval of the '60s and '70s was supposed to have changed the roles governing the sexes.

> But the truth is that, while the rules may have changed, the roles all too often remain firmly in place. For example, today men may be willing to concede that women are as rational as they, and women may claim they welcome men who are unashamed of crying. But, when it comes to who is responsible for raising the kids and who should make the most money in the family, things tend to remain much the same. Traits may be interchangeable, but the roles are not.[7]

The reasons behind Mrs. P's anger at her husband were real as well as complex. However, there is no doubt that she was deeply disappointed that he did not fulfill the traditional expectations for men. Internalized racism by both Mrs. P and Mr. P complicated the problem. The internalized racism was in their both adopting wider society sex role expectations at the expense of more flexible roles related to their actual needs;[8] that is, stereotypical male and female roles emphasize male dominance and female submissiveness while there are many more flexible roles that facilitate male and female mutuality.

Mr. P and Mrs. P represented two prominent theories of racism. One theory is that racism is determinative, and the other school is that racism is a given that can be overcome through connectedness with racial and cultural resources. It has been pointed out that the approach that is taken to racism is often determined by gender in the African American community. Katie Cannon, in *Black Womanist Ethics*, points out that African American male writers tend to focus on the conflict and confrontation between the white and the black worlds. African American female writers, however, concentrate more intensely on the community and the relationships within them.[9] She goes on to indicate that African American women writers embrace the narrative oral culture that hands down moral and religious rules through folk culture.[10] The point is that African American men and women, as exemplified by Mr. and Mrs. P, view racism differently.

My own bias is related to recognizing that being emotionally connected across generations is the key factor in African Americans' successfully coming to grips with racism historically. I fully believe that Billingsley's research concerning how African American families have survived is accurate. It is being relationally connected to the cultural heritage through cross-generational relationships that has made the difference for African American families. Moreover, Lena Wright Myers also points out that cross-generational contact is a real key in the way African American men handle racism. Her research reveals that many African American men in her sample felt that despite negative evaluations of the roles of black men in society, the majority believed that black men played important roles in their positive socialization. In other words, fathers, grandfathers, older male siblings, uncles, cousins, and surrogate male parents participated positively in their upbringing.[11] This was key to their survival in society.

Racism played an important role in the marital and family life of Mr. and Mrs. P. How they responded to racial discrimination fell along gender lines. However, the family connectedness for them has not been explored. This will be done later in the chapter. The purpose of this section was to lift up how racism was a stressor and its impact on African American marriages and families.

From the point of view of the liberated growth norm and the love ethic, the key is for the family and family members to respond to racism in ways that facilitate the growth of each family member. It was obvious that Mr. P wanted Mrs. P to sacrifice her own well-being to fulfill his needs for support. Her refusal to do this was interpreted as desertion by Mr. P. She realized that if she was going to survive in the marriage, she would have to focus more on her own growth spiritually and vocationally. Mr. P saw this as selfishness and felt this was not the proper role for women to play. The question is, Where did the ideas that were influencing their views of male and female roles come from? This is the subject of the next section.

Religious Views

Mr. and Mrs. P have been influenced by propositional theological views regarding male and female relationships. This means that they have developed ideal images of what a marriage is and what roles each spouse is to play within their relationship. Their ideal marriage or marital mythology focuses on the religious view that the man is to be the benevolent head of the household while the woman is supposed to be the willing follower.

They both have accepted this ideal image without challenging it. However, Mrs. P is steadily realizing that her growth needs and needs for *self-differentiation*, or a sense of self apart from her marriage partner, are being frustrated by trying to reach this ideal marital image. She is slowly coming to the awareness that she was naive to put her whole life in the hands of her husband thinking that he could handle this better than she. She was becoming resentful that she had to sacrifice more of herself to fulfill this ideal image than Mr. P had to sacrifice. She would, however, retain this marital image of headship if Mr. P were better able to be more responsible with her dependence on him. She expected that he should be able to take more responsibility for her growth and development. She found it hard to take more responsibility for her own growth.

Mr. P was very uncomfortable with Mrs. P's effort to become more responsible for herself and her own unhappiness. He was very comfortable with her remaining totally dependent on him. He found her effort toward differentiating herself or knowing who she was apart from him to be very threatening to him. Therefore, he relied on traditional religious values to remind her who the head of the house was. To be head of the house meant that he would make all the money, make all the major decisions, and that his job would take precedence over her job. He expected her to be supportive of him in every way without questioning his adequacy.

This propositional view of the ideal marriage has connections to the way African Americans have learned religious values. First, research into the African American church reveals that African American Christians tend to be orthodox theologically even though they have different degrees of emphasis with regard to social and racial issues.[12] A critical religious difference between the African American Christian worldview and that of wider Christian culture is the emphasis that African American Christians place on the incarnational view of suffering, the belief in social and economic freedom, the God who is involved in history, and the biblical view of the importance of the human personality and human equality before God.[13] Yet, accompanying these liberal social views regarding freedom, there is a belief in a form of religious patriarchalism that can be seen within African American churches.

Delores Aldridge traces African American patriarchy to racism and sexism of wider American culture. For her racism is the systematic denial and deformation of a people's history and humanity rooted in racial hierarchies.[14] She defines *sexism* as gender and/or sex hierarchies as the basis for determining and justifying relationships and exchanges.[15] In addition to racism and sexism, she also points out that black males and females embrace a Judeo-Christian ethic that enshrines male aggressiveness within a narrowly defined leadership style, and defines femininity as submission to males.[16] She goes on to say that racism, sexism, and the Judeo-Christian

ethic directly impact male and female relationships and reinforce feelings
of inferiority for both African American males and females. However,
African American females get a double dose of inferiority. She points out
that African Americans, on the whole, seem to have bought into the patriarchal beliefs of the wider culture. In my own research, this seems to have
been more the case when African American males saw that they could become men like white men as the result of the civil rights struggle.[17] This
basically means that black men feel they must identify with patriarchy in
order to be regarded as real men.

Delores Williams traces the contemporary religious views of male and
female relationships to the postbellum African American society. In *Sisters
in the Wilderness*, she points out that during this time African American men
tended to imitate whites by keeping their wives and daughters at home.
Some African American women also reported that they wanted to be supported by their husbands the way white men supported their wives.[18] She
comments: "Both black men and black women were obviously trying to pattern black family life after the patriarchal model of family sanctioned in
mainline America."[19] The end result, in Williams's mind, was that African
American women began to subscribe to a view of femininity that made them
relinquish roles that put them in less threatening roles than black men. As
a consequence, black women became proficient in women's work.

In the last section internalized racism was related to traditional sex roles.
The point was that stereotypical sex roles become part of racism in that
African Americans often place higher values on what wider society deems
the norm. Yet this way of assigning value to things can be very damaging
to African Americans, especially to women. Renita Weems explores one aspect of exaggerated femininity that she calls the Leah Syndrome, which is
based on Leah in the Old Testament.

> The Leah Syndrome refers to women who love too much, women who
> conspire against themselves in relationships, women who refuse to let go,
> women who use their sexuality to snare men they're better off without,
> women who allow what the men in their lives think of them to become
> what they think of themselves, women who get involved in relationships
> that are a re-creation of painful memories from their childhoods.[20]

Weems goes on to say that Leah's story is about a woman who went to
great lengths in order to get her husband to love her. However, in order to
accomplish her goal she had to sacrifice her self in the process. Weems concludes that the Leahs of today are relationship addicts:

> Relationship addicts do not have husbands or lovers; they have hostages.
> Their self-esteem is tied to their relationship. Relationship addicts never
> let go of past relationships, and when the present one is on the rocks an-

other one is always in the making. Relationship addicts are obsessed about their lack of a relationship, and they will do anything to stay in a relationship, find a relationship. A pseudo-relationship is better than no relationship.[21]

The point is that the Leah Syndrome combined with religious patriarchy and internalized racism causes women to lose their identities. This syndrome causes women to love men who cannot return the love.[22] Some women wake up, and this was precisely the place that Mrs. P found herself. The reality of her husband's limitations was forcing her to examine her own situation and state.

While patriarchy has deep roots within African American traditional religion, it must not be concluded that this was the only tradition of male and female relationships within the African American community. There is a rich tradition of male and female egalitarianism and androgyny going back to African roots, slavery, and its aftermath where African American men and women worked together as equals in order to survive racism and oppression.[23] However, this tradition has been abandoned by many men largely because of identification with wider cultural images of masculinity and femininity.

As a consequence of this patriarchal history traditional religious views of male and female relationships permeate African American religious circles today. Many African American couples attend Christian marital enrichment groups that emphasize traditional male and female roles. Some black churches are now training African Americans in biblical counseling that focus on traditional roles. In fact, one study was done of seventy-five African American couples, and the results showed that most of these marriages preferred tradition-led homes. Clarence Walker, an African American Christian therapist who reported this finding, says:

> My practice, which involves hundreds of hours as a marriage counselor, with a case load of ninety percent black Christian couples, supports the finding of Gray-Little. Born again black couples tend to prefer the husband-led home taught in Ephesians 5. While this evidence is not conclusive, it does show that a segment of the black population finds satisfaction in marriages that establish traditional homes according to Judeo-Christian values.[24]

Walker goes on to say that black male headship of the family seems to be related to how well black males can fulfill the traditional expectations of masculinity. This means being able to support the family well and being sensitive and caring. He does say that many of the marriages that actually function well under male leadership are the ones that are egalitarian in which female needs are respected.[25]

My own counseling practice also supports what Walker says about preference for a form of egalitarian headship. I think that Mrs. P would prefer a modified form of male headship in the home where the husband was more responsible and sensitive to her needs. However, theologically I am pushed to go beyond what African American couples find comfortable in relating to each other from the theological norm of holistic growth and the ethic of love. How do these theological principles relate to traditional patriarchy that seems to be a preferred model for many African American Christians?

Theologically, it is important to evaluate the traditional notions of male headship and female submission in light of the norm of holistic growth and the ethic of love. It must be remembered that the eschatological community was one that was lived between the ages in egalitarian ways. Each person had a significant role to play in this community regardless of gender. This egalitarian participation, then, became the norm for participation in families and marriages for the sake of the unfolding rule of God. Consequently, the egalitarian principle became the guide for all human relationships and on which all relationships had to be evaluated.

This means that no propositional ideal image of marriage is baptized as the model. Rather, the emphasis is on process and dynamics, in terms of how a family and marriage lives in ways that free its members for full participation in God's unfolding reign. Consequently, the structures of families and marriages change to meet the needs of family members and marital partners. Moreover, the structures of marriages and families change so that each family member can find ways to discover his or her vocation in God's salvation drama.

This model of dynamic and process-oriented family life, compared to the propositional structural model of family and marital life, puts marital and family relationships within a larger theological perspective. The goal of the marriage and family life is not just personal, but inclusive of marital and family satisfaction where all persons grow and develop into their full possibilities as God's people. These are important goals. However, these goals are means to the ultimate end. The ultimate end is a vocational one where marital partners and family members discern their vocational work and role in God's salvation drama. Consequently, there is a relationship between the growth of each family member and the coming of God's reign on earth. Each marriage and family must create the kind of flexible pattern that permits them to respond to the vocation that each family member has in God's salvation drama.

When this idea of a process and dynamic model of marital and family life is applied to Mr. and Mrs. P, it does appear that their marriage and family structure and marriage and family process are hindrances to the growth and development of each family member. They are not conducive to producing the kind of growth needed to move them toward their ultimate vocational objectives.

Pastoral counseling with Mr. and Mrs. P would involve helping them to create the kind of marriage and family that freed each family member to find his or her vocation in God's unfolding drama of salvation. This means attending to the kinds of things in their relationship that hinder such an attainment and attending to the external factors that produce stress in their marital relationship. Therefore, the pastoral counselor needs to give attention to bicultural pressures, racial discrimination, and religious values. The goal is to improve the quality of marital and family functioning for the sake of the rule of God.

Chapter Four

A Transgenerational View

The external context influencing the worldview of African American marriages and families involves bicultural concerns, racial factors, and the influence of religious values and themes. In addition, other forces within marriages and families help to shape the worldview and values of African American marriages and families. As families and marriages move from generation to generation, they develop patterns for responding to life crises and life transitions. These are passed on from generation to generation and are called vertical patterns.[1]

These *vertical patterns* are family myths, family legacies, family secrets, and inherited family interaction patterns. They help families and marriages respond to predictable transitions related to individual, marital, and family life cycles, as well as those changes caused by unpredictable events confronting the family.

Social and cultural forces combine with vertical patterns and influence the worldview and values that African Americans bring to pastoral counseling. Understanding these multiple factors and their impact on African American marriages and families is essential for appropriate marital and family assessment and intervention.

A central theological concern of this chapter is to relate the norm of holistic growth and the ethic of love governing the eschatological community to a multigenerational view of African American marriages and families; that is, the holistic growth norm and ethic of love have multigenerational impact on the lives of family members. Consequently, attending to the growth of each marital partner and the growth and development of each family member has ramifications for generations to come. This means that pastoral counseling with African American marriages and families can set the stage for influencing future generations.

An additional theological concern is how to evaluate growth-facilitating and growth-inhibiting cross-generational patterns. The norm of holistic growth and the ethic of love understood in the biblical community's concept of the eschatological community will be used to this end. The ministry concern is to help release the growth-facilitating dimensions of marriages and families for the well-being of future generations as well as for the coming of God's rule on earth.

Mr. and Mrs. P
and Parentified Childhoods

Previously depicted was that Mr. P and Mrs. P were given parental authority prematurely. Mr. P's mother got very ill, and he had to assume the role of caregiver for his younger brothers and sisters. Mrs. P also was forced into adult responsibility because she felt her mother had abdicated her parental role. Both Mr. P. and Mrs. P were the oldest in terms of sibling position and both were parentified children. That is, they were given the responsibility to take care of younger siblings.[2] In both cases this allocation was maladaptive because it led to parental abdication in both families.

Both Mr. and Mrs. P experienced their parental roles as oppressive. They believed that they lost their childhoods as a result. Of significance is the fact that many of the patterns associated with their families of birth were repeated or rebelled against in their current marriage. Mr. P rebelled against taking adult responsibility within his family of creation feeling that he was deprived of his childhood. Mrs. P, however, conformed to her family of origin pattern by becoming the caretaker of her husband and two children. She experienced such caretaking as oppressive and desired to be out from under this pressure.

Note the vertical pattern: family of origin legacies affecting every interaction that was undertaken within the family. *Family legacies* are those interactive patterns that are handed down from generation to generation within families.[3] Such legacies can be either growth-facilitating or growth-inhibiting. In the case of Mr. and Mrs. P, they were definitely nongrowth-producing.

The multigenerational legacy of being parentified children needs to be examined in light of the external forces of race, biculturalism, and religious values. Parentified children are not unique to African Americans. Because of such external factors as race, bicultural consideration, and religious values, however, parentified children seem to be a major factor in many African American families.[4]

Race in the United States refers to the history of racism and its influence on the lives of African Americans and other racially identifiable groups. Racism is an ideology that espouses that black people are inferior and less than human. This belief served as a facilitating rationale that allowed white Americans to disrupt and destroy African American families for the sake of slavery and for capitalism after slavery. Racism made African American family life secondary.

During slavery African American families were broken and separated by selling children, parents, and spouses like animals. The industrial and technological revolution followed slavery. Racism kept African Americans at the lower end of the economic scale as a major source of cheap labor. Because of economic exploitation and racial discrimination both parents usually had to work to make a meager living for the family. Moreover, unemployment, particularly among males in the cities, forced many males from the home. Whether both parents worked or whether unemployment forced men from the home, the end result was that older children were left to care for younger children. The oldest child became the parental substitute.[5]

Another unique dimension for African Americans is that either males or females are parentified. This is different from some other ethnic groups in which the oldest female becomes the parentified child.[6]

Mr. and Mrs. P were oldest children and were parentified, being assigned parental roles as children. This disrupted their personal growth and became a major source for their marital and family discord. Their parentified roles were emotionally devastating to them because their parents abdicated their parental roles. In functional African American families, children are given the parental roles on a temporary basis and only when the parents are not home. When the parent comes home, however, the child relinquishes the role and the parent assumes the responsibility. In contrast, parents in dysfunctional families completely abdicate. This was the case for both Mr. and Mrs. P.

Parentified children in dysfunctional families often give up their childhoods. This was especially the case with Mr. P. Because he felt deprived of a childhood, he developed a feeling of entitlement. He feels he is entitled to be taken care of by others because of his lost childhood. Consequently, he abdicates his adult role in his family of creation.

Mrs. P did not have the same privilege of abdicating adult responsibility that Mr. P had. Although she was a parentified child the African American worldview emphasizes the role of the mother in child-rearing. Boyd-Franklin says that black mothers who work and raise children have a strong tradition of self-reliance.[7] Many African American mothers grow up with good role models provided by their aunts, mothers, and grandmothers. Despite their working outside the home, many take their home parenting role very seriously. Therefore, a long tradition of responsible African American female parents undergirds the way Mrs. P sees her parenting role. She feels she has no choice other than to be a responsible adult parent. She did, however, have feelings of resentment, depression, and exhaustion as a result. While African American men are also expected to be mature and responsible adults, they have no lasting tradition of expectations that is similar to the one for African American women.

Religious values also reinforce the mother role of African American women. The duties of mothers are emphasized in most black churches. The traditional yearly observance of Mother's Day in African American churches is the best-attended Sunday worship service except for perhaps Easter. At this service the virtues of mothers are extolled and celebrated. People like Mrs. P would be fully aware of these values and internalize them for her behavior.

Another influence on the Ps' marriage can be noted. *Biculturalism* refers to living in two cultures simultaneously. It also refers to making a primary commitment to one and a secondary commitment to the other. From a gender perspective African American women tend to be committed to the values related to their ethnic and racial culture more than to wider culture.[8] African American men, however, tend to be more oriented toward wider culture. These two generalizations are true in the cases of Mr. and Mrs. P. Mrs. P's values relate more to her cultural heritage while Mr. P's values resemble the wider culture. Because of this Mrs. P is locked into the role of responsible parent, and Mr. P takes more latitude to escape the home and its parenting responsibility.

When their family legacies are evaluated from the standpoint of the norm of holistic growth and the ethic of love, it is clear that they are living in nongrowth-facilitating ways. Consequently, they need to find ways with more meaningful patterns.

Transgenerational Family Theory

A major problem for African American families, whether oriented toward the racial or wider culture, is the potential emotional cutoff. This dangerous possibility arises because American society is oriented toward isolating individuals from community. The concept of *emotional cutoff* introduced by Murray Bowen in 1975 describes emotional processes that exist between the generations.[9] This process depicts how people deal with their emotional attachment to previous generations. Self-differentiation, for Bowen, is a process of becoming a self apart from others while still maintaining emotional connectedness with one's parents and previous generations. Connectedness with past generations needs to be maintained if an individual is to become truly self-differentiated. Indeed, the family that remains in healthy emotional contact with past generations is emotionally healthier than the family that does not maintain this contact. Emotionally cutoff people find themselves and their families perpetually stuck in the life cycle transitions.

Boyd-Franklin examines the significance of emotional cutoffs for African American families.[10] Some black families that achieve middle-class status may often find themselves emotionally cut off from their families of origin. Many black families have sacrificed so that others in the family could achieve middle-class status. The sacrificing family expects that the professional black person who achieves middle-class status will return to extended family members with financial, emotional, and physical resources. This is viewed as only a fair exchange for what the family sacrificed. The choices for many black professionals are either to continue to participate in this form of extended family obligatory reciprocity system or to isolate themselves from it. Those who isolate themselves from it are viewed as ungrateful traitors.

On the surface, such family exchange expectations may not be different from expectations from Euro-Americans. Ethnic groups in general seem to have extended family expectations related to success. Consequently, the exchange orientation is similar for most intact ethnic groups in the United States. The point is that, given the nature of the dependence on the extended family for survival in the African American community, cutoffs are particularly dangerous.

Boyd-Franklin talks about the therapeutic implication of this either-or choice facing some middle-class African American families. She lifts up the fact that severe psychological consequences occur when the self is isolated from the extended family. But such consequences also occur when the person is unwillingly giving in to the obligatory reciprocal system. If the family who has achieved middle-class status attempts to stay connected with extended-family members, class conflict often arises with those family members who have not achieved this status. Superiority and inferiority feelings may be generated. This often intensifies the desire for emotional cutoffs by the family that achieved middle-class status. Such cutoffs leave family members psychologically vulnerable, with meager resources for dealing with life's problems. The remedy is to help the family who achieves middle-class status in managing contact with extended families and families of origin.

In my clinical experience many African Americans find this either-or choice very intimidating. It threatens individual and family feelings of well-being. Many do not know whether to give into the pressure to assume the obligatory reciprocity system and give up middle-class status or to cut themselves off from the family of origin. My intervention strategy with those who are intimidated by this vicelike pressure is to help them to return home and maintain emotional contact with the family of origin and extended family while working not to give in to pressures that they feel are inappropriate. I emphasize responding to family needs in ways that do not jeopardize their own sense of personal and family of creation integrity and well-being.

From a theological perspective, emotional cutoff cannot serve the ends of the norm of holistic growth and the ethic of love. Connectedness across generations can be facilitative of growth. However, it could be detrimental to growth. The concept of emotional cutoff helps the pastoral counselor have practical handles for evaluating how healthy the cross-generational connections are. Armed with specifics the pastoral counselor can also work with people to make healthy contact with the families of birth and origin to assure their own growth and well-being. This concept can help them to modify the growth-debilitating dimensions of connecting to the family of origin.

Differentiation and Multigenerational Transmission Process

Connecting to the family of origin is not all positive, and some real dangers need to be addressed. Boyd-Franklin addresses these concerns by drawing on several important Bowenian concepts, including differentiation and the multigenerational transmission process.[11]

Differentiation of self refers to a sense of self apart from others. This term does not mean isolated autonomy where a person achieves an emotional cutoff. Rather, it refers to a sense of self while being connected to the family of origin. Boyd-Franklin points out that the extended family orientation of African American families may make it difficult for some individuals to achieve individuation or self-differentiation. She says that some of these families frankly fear individuation, particularly if the persons are moving up the economic and class ladder.[12] This connection of self-differentiation and class mobility may leave the person without extended-family support, and emotional symptoms may emerge in those who are differentiating. She views emotional cutoffs, then, as psychological suicide. Moreover, because extended-family relationships have been so important to African Americans, emotional cutoffs between one generation and earlier generations could also have an impact for generations to come.[13]

People who achieve a good sense of differentiation generally pass this self-differentiation on to the next generation, *multigenerational transmission process*. Michael Kerr and Murray Bowen define this process as the process of transmitting relational patterns from one generation to the next.[14] These relational patterns can be functional and facilitate the self-differentiation of the next generation, or they can be dysfunctional and hinder the development of self-differentiation in the next generation.

Boyd-Franklin focuses on the multigenerational transmission process in African American families that produces impairment in children.[15] She highlights the ways in which family anxiety focuses around certain family secrets that surround the birth of children. These secrets often involve paternity and skin color differences. For example, some children are different shades of color, and this raises some questions about who might be the father of the child. She also uses the concept of family repetitions to refer to relational problems and anxiety that repeat themselves in one generation after another to describe how family secrets impact the next generation. What usually happens is that similar problems surrounding birth reappear in the next generation at similar times that they appeared in the previous generation.

Multigenerational problems not only reappear in the next generation in the offspring but also within the marital relationship as well. Boyd-Franklin explores the multigenerational transmission process issues in black couples.[16] Black couples also repeat family of origin patterns in their relationships with their mates. Often, unresolved problems with the family of origin get repeated in the marriage and cause a great deal of conflict. For example, Mr. and Mrs. P have marital difficulty rooted in the fact that they were parentified children. Kerr and Bowen say that this kind of repetition is the result of people with similar levels of self-differentiation usually marrying each other. Thus, those who have low levels of self-differentiation are more vulnerable to repeat the dysfunctional patterns from their family of origin.[17]

My own experience as a pastoral marriage and family therapist with African Americans is that the role people played in the family of origin often gets played out in marital relationships. Low self-differentiation means that the person has not gotten enough freedom from the family of origin roles to choose different roles in new relationships. The person is still locked into playing this role or its opposite, and this lack of freedom permeates the new relationships. Persons of similar low levels of differentiation usually come into reactive conflict because their lack of freedom generally complements the other spouse's lack of freedom.

Self-differentiation, like the concept of emotional cutoff, serves the end of holistic growth and the ethic of love. Self-differentiation defined in this context is not growth at the expense of another. Rather, it is growth of self while facilitating the growth of others. When the growth of others is as important as the growth of self, then, the growth norm and the ethic of love are operative.

African American Male and Female Relations in Transgenerational Perspective

Several important issues face African American marriages and families that need to be put in a transgenerational perspective. One such issue is black female and male relationships.

Delores Aldridge has studied black male and female relationships in depth.[18] Capitalism, racism, sexism, and the Judeo-Christian ethic are factors that intensify the separation from family roots and make it easier to become emotionally isolated from the extended-family roots and values.[19] These factors need to be placed with transgenerational theory.

With regard to capitalism, the pursuit of profit and private ownership has a tremendous impact on behavior of human beings and their interactions with others. Pressures, for example, to exchange past relationships for marketplace values is much related to the development of capitalism. Socialization in a capitalist society and giving of the self totally to it can have a devastating impact on black male and female relationships; for example, being uprooted for the sake of following one's job and moving to a faraway town adds stress to the lives of men and women.

Racism is a systematic denial and deformation of people's history and humanity rooted in hierarchies of race.[20] Sexism is defined as male gender and/or sex as the primary determinant in establishing and justifying relationships.[21] Racism makes people denigrate their past, and sexism lifts up the male gender as superior. The Judeo-Christian tradition can promote and reinforce black and white female inferior positions by reinforcing racism and sexism.[22] These four factors according to Aldridge have a direct impact on black male and female relationships. Uncritical assimilation into the dominant culture's values does a great deal to contaminate the relationships between black males and females.

Drawing on her analysis of the pressures impacting black male and female relationships, Aldridge examines their relationships in more detail. She makes several conclusions after reviewing the research. First, black male and female relationships are no more problem-ridden than other male and female relationships.[23] Second, many black male and female relationships are healthy; however, there are many that are not. Third, she feels that it is important to look carefully at those relationships that are not healthy. Fourth, she feels that the following factors influence the quality of black male and female relationships: the scarcity of black men, differential socialization of males and females, sexism and women's liberation, and modes of connecting.[24]

The scarcity of black men complicates the relationship between black males and females because this often pits black women against each other, and it forces black women to accept black males on black males' own terms.[25] This scarcity is complicated by the sexism of black males where they also accept the dominant sexist images of masculinity and femininity.

One of the most devastating problems existing between African American males and females relates to the differential socialization of males and females in society.[26] Dominant societal images of masculinity define the male role as being tough, objective, striving, achieving, unsentimental, and emotionally unexpressive. Aldridge feels that this image of what it means to be male in wider society forces black men to mask their true feelings, and makes it very difficult for them to achieve empathy with black women. She points out that many black women want emotional expressiveness and intimate relationships with men. They want expressions of gentleness, tenderness, and verbal affection. Yet, black women expect black men to be strong, unexpressive, and cool. This often leads to confusion and contradictions for both black males and females. Some men feel that expressions of emotions leave them vulnerable. Aldridge responds to this dilemma by suggesting that black males and females need to measure manhood, particularly, by the standards of responsiveness, support, care, and honesty. She says that black women can help black men by encouraging them to express their feelings rather than to conceal them.

How feelings and emotional expressiveness take place between black males and females is of crucial significance to many couples that I have seen in pastoral counseling. Aldridge's analysis of the problems related to emotional expressiveness are supported by my clinical experience. In fact, when black males and females are married for any length of time, many black women want more emotional and verbal expressiveness. When black men fail to respond to this need for emotional expressiveness and affection, this often leads to anger and feelings of rejection and abandonment by black women. Many black wives feel unappreciated and are deeply angry. Black men respond by trying to do some activity to please their wives that is consistent with their image of being male. However, the emotional expressiveness demands can only be met through the quality of being present and empathic to the female rather than a lot of activity. Pastoral counseling can help men see the needs of women for a quality of presence and empathy rather than concrete "doing."

Aldridge feels that these enumerated problems between black males and females are value-oriented and rooted in the foundation of American society.[27] She feels that many black males and females accept these values uncritically, and the goals of any program to address black male and female relationships should begin with a study of the values that help shape their relationships.

I agree that addressing the problems between black males and females is a valuable issue. Uncritical assimilation into dominant societal values regarding life is indeed problem laden. However, the way that this book seeks to lead pastoral counselors working with African American marriages and families is to help people in these relationships to become bicultural. That is, the goal of biculturalism is to help people stay deeply rooted in their cultural and religious heritage of values while participating in wider culture for the purposes of economic survival. The pastoral counselor needs to help African Americans to clarify the values that they strive to achieve in wider society, and correlate them with the cultural heritage of values that support extended-family and religious values. Such an approach needs to help those in African American marriages and families to appropriate those values that enhance their connectedness and mutual nurturing of family members and marital partners.

The bicultural issue raised in relationship to African American male and female relationships is also a theological issue. One of the important dimensions of the eschatological community is that participation in it did not mean that one had to deny or set aside one's cultural heritage.[28] Inclusion in the eschatological community was not dependent on ethnic background or gender. Rather, it was based on invitation and whether the invitation was responded to positively. Therefore, it is important to evaluate assimilation into dominant culture and its accompanying values in light of the biblical eschatological community.

An important theological issue related to biculturalism has to do with connectedness across generations, and this issue has been raised by womanist pastoral theologian Carolyn McCrary. Being connected across generations is a transgenerational orientation and is related to the concept of interdependence in the thinking of McCrary. For her, interdependence is a theological norm for pastoral theological formulations. She understands interdependence to be a cross-generational experience involving individual psychological factors, several generations within the family, relationships with community, and personal responsibility.[29] For McCrary, interdependence is being connected with community and others in important ways, while at the same time taking full responsibility for one's own life.

Of significance in McCrary's work is the fact that she does not make any gender distinctions between interdependency and the roles of black males and females. She describes interdependency as a norm to which both males and females need to adhere as if there were not any real gender differences between males and females when it comes to interdependence.

Interdependence understood cross-generationally is also important for understanding the historic and theological sources of African American manhood. The sources of manhood include the African heritage, the African American tradition of male and female egalitarian relationships and androgynous roles, the penchant for oral styles of communication, the use of the theological resources of Bible stories and characters.[30]

In addition to the above, other theological issues are important. It is important to see the issues of sexism in African American male and female relationships as violating the norm of liberated growth and the ethic of love. Moreover, treating potential mates and spouses as sexual objects without consideration of the well-being of the other does not contribute to the growth of either. Adopting dominant societal images of masculinity and femininity also seems to hinder the growth of both males and females. Conforming exclusively to marketplace values seems to frustrate the growth of families as well. However, cross-generational connectedness and being rooted in the religious and value heritage of the past seems to serve the ends of the norm of liberated growth and the ethic of love. The African American religious and cultural heritage has close roots to the understanding of the biblical eschatological community developed here, and it can be used in service of the growth and development of marital partners and family members.

Single-Parent Black Families

Another multigenerational issue relates to the single-parent family. Boyd-Franklin refers to the startling increase in black female-headed households. She says that this trend has emerged in the last decade and parallels a similar trend in all North American families.[31]

While there are similar trends existing in all North American families, she warns against treating such families as dysfunctional. She says that there are functional and dysfunctional single-parent black families. These families include a variety of family structures: (1) single and never married, (2) single, divorced or separated, and (3) single, widowed.[32]

It is important to place single-parent families within a transgenerational perspective to shed light on the differences between functional and dysfunctional single-parent black families. Functional single-parent families have the following functional characteristics: (1) roles and responsibilities are well delineated and age appropriate; (2) boundaries between generations are clear but flexible; (3) children have easy access to the parent; (4) both parent and children receive nurturing and communicate their own needs; (5) there may be a parentified child to carry some of the adult responsibility, but the parent has not abdicated parental responsibility; (6) single parents have a life of their own apart from the children; and (7) the single-parent family utilizes the extended-family support system.[33] This latter point means that the single-parent families that maintain good extended-family relationships and cross-generational ties function quite well.

Boyd-Franklin points out that there are several kinds of dysfunctional single-parent black families. They include those that are the underorganized; those with an overcentralized overburdened parent; those with a dysfunctional parent and a parentified child running the family; those with a hidden member of the family; and the three-generation family that has dysfunctional patterns.[34]

In dysfunctional single-parent black families, extended family involvement is erratic, unpredictable, destabilizing, and nonsupportive.[35] These families tend to be emotionally cut off from extended-family support. Without such support it is often hard for the parent to assume executive responsibility within the family.

Boyd-Franklin also points out that dysfunctional patterns in single-parent families can also be symptomatic of extended-family dysfunctional problems.[36] Significant in these families was the fact that there was either isolation from or death of a significant extended-family member that had been a source of emotional and financial support.[37] The death of a grand-mother or mother in three-generation homes could be disastrous. The key point is that extended-family support is essential for single-parent families to survive and function well.

Theologically, for pastoral counselors to seek cross-generational connectedness is very important to the growth and development of family members. Cross-generational connectedness in growth-facilitating ways can serve the ends of liberated growth and the ethic of love. Pastoral counselors must help people in single-parent families explore ways that they can be connected cross-generationally or become part of a caring community that is multigenerational.

Summary

The transgenerational model is valuable because it helps the pastoral counselor to place families and their problems that are presented by individuals, couples, and families in the context of transgenerational forces.[38] The emphasis is on the fact that family problems as well as family strengths do not develop suddenly, but have a history that may be multigenerational. The value of the transgenerational perspective is that it enables the pastoral counselor to trace family development over a period of time. It also enables the people facing the problem to see it in a broader context that might enable them to reframe the problem and take pressure off the immediate situation.

One major assumption undergirding this chapter is that positive consequences result when people reconnect with their extended families and families of origin. This is a viable option even when the extended family or family of origin was dysfunctional. Persons who come from dysfunctional families of origin, however, should reconnect with these families without adopting the dysfunctional roles and activities that once characterized their lives. Rather, visits that are coached by a pastoral counselor for the purposes of self-differentiation are recommended. This means that persons should only return home while in therapy so that the person receives feedback and support. The chief goal for such reconnecting is to be the adult self even in the presence of undermining patterns.

Theologically, it is also possible to expand on the biblical understanding of the eschatological community, its norm of liberated growth and the ethic of love, and the norm of interdependence. Liberated growth and

development and affirming the growth and development of marital partners and family members involves being connected across generations in
ways that nurture the marriage and family to perform its growth-liberating
function. The value of the cross-generational perspective is that it helps us
envisage how being connected across generations helps to free marriages
and families from isolation and can offer support as they seek to perform
their liberating growth and loving functions.

Chapter Five

The Horizontal Context: The Life Cycle

Life cycle rhythms are very important to African American marriages and families. In fact, the inherited African worldview took very seriously the life of the community centered around the transitions in the life cycle, such as birth, naming children, rites of passage of children into adulthood, rites of passage for the dying, and others. The point is that the life cycle perspective is not new to African Americans.

What is new, however, is the fact that modern living has impacted the life cycle of human beings in phenomenal ways; for example, retirement, divorce, adult life cycles, and parents living past the launching of children have become part of the modern life cycle. The question could be raised, then, What is the significance of contemporary life cycle theory for African American marriages and families? Is the life cycle of African Americans different from that of other groups? If so, how?

Another important dimension of a life cycle perspective is how the life cycle relates to a cross-generational perspective. When one puts African American marriages and families and life cycle transitions into a cross-generational perspective, the result is that multiple life cycles come into perspective. That is to say, there are individual life cycles, marital life cycles, and family life cycles. In a three-generation life cycle model, one would need to explore the individual, marital, and family life cycles in each generation to understand the human beings involved. The intent here is to look at the various levels of the life cycle in African American marriages and families and to demonstrate how a life cycle perspective can enrich what is done in pastoral counseling with this group of people.

The relevance of life cycle theories in general for African Americans is that they have utility in organizing life span material and describing developmental changes within the life cycle of African Americans.[1] The crucial difficulty with these general theories, however, is that they are usually developed on middle-class white men, and these studies tend to become normative and distort the experiences of African Americans.[2] With this limitation acknowledged it is possible to move to clinical material and writings by some African Americans to understand life cycles and African Americans.

The Case of Mr. and Mrs. P

As you will remember, Mr. P is forty-five and Mrs. P is thirty-seven years of age. They have two boys ages three and twelve. In addition to this, Mr. P has an aging mother and Mrs. P has aging parents. This means that at least three generations make up the extended family in their lives. Not only this, but at least three or four life cycles are present in their multi-generational family. These life cycles include (1) extended-family life cycles, (2) family life cycles, (3) marital life cycles, and (4) individual life cycles at each generational stage. When the family of Mr. and Mrs. P is analyzed in light of these divergent life cycles, many hidden factors about their marital relationship and family life surface and give added perspective to their relationship difficulties.

Examples of how the life cycle gives added perspective to their relational difficulties are important. Mr. and Mrs. P are in the expansion stage of the family life cycle. This means that they have expanded their marital dyad to include children. Second, each child and each parent has his or her own individual life cycle. The three-year-old is in the early childhood stage; the twelve-year-old is in the preadolescent stage; Mr. P is in the midlife stage; Mrs. P is nearing the midlife stage but is still in the period of consolidating her adult identity; both Mr. and Mrs. P have parents that could one day be dependent on them; and Mr. P has one child from a previous marriage. What all of these different stages mean is that there are multiple life cycles present in their family. Each life cycle stage has particular tasks that need to be accomplished. Understanding these different stages and the various tasks is significant when trying to get conceptual and practical handles on what is taking place in the relationship between Mr. and Mrs. P. Putting their marital difficulty into a life cycle perspective is crucial.

One key to understanding their marital problem is related to the different individual life cycle stages of Mr. and Mrs. P. Moreover, there are some gender differences in life cycles that impinge upon the problem. Mrs. P went from her parents' home into the marriage and now wants some self-differentiation space. Mr. P responds to this as a threat to losing her. This forces him to want to control her. Moreover, Mr. P belongs to a different life cycle and has little sympathy for the life cycle tasks of Mrs. P. She has not begun midlife and has very little understanding of his life cycle tasks. They also have an expanding family, and this adds stress to the family.

There are several distinct life cycles operative in this case study. From an individual life cycle perspective Mr. and Mrs. P are at different individual stages of their individual development. In terms of their marital life cycle, they are expanding their lives to include children, and they are at the expansion stage of family development. Their individual, marital, and family stages of development call them to perform specific tasks in order to adjust to these stages. Moreover, the marital problem facing Mr. and Mrs. P has roots in the multiple life cycle challenges they face. This brief placing of the marital problem in the life cycle gives insight into their problem and suggests that both need to be aware of the life cycle issues and tasks that each is undergoing.

The Life Cycle Perspective and African American Marriages and Families

One way to extricate African Americans from the middle-class white male-oriented life cycle is to attend to the cultural and racial factors that influence how African Americans traverse these stages of the life cycle.

African Americans have inherited an African philosophy of harmony with nature that influences how African Americans negotiate the developmental life cycle.[3] African philosophy emphasizes the natural rhythm of nature and human beings in cooperation with nature.[4] Illustrative of this is the coordination of the religious and ritual life of the African community with rites of transition at key stages of the life cycle. The rites of transition serve to renew individuals and their communities.

Rhythms of nature involve the seasons of nature.[5] Human life envisaged is dynamically related to and analogous with the rhythms of nature. Therefore, days, weeks, years, and seasons of life are very important. There are the rhythms of birth, puberty, initiation into adulthood, marriage, procreation, old age, and death. Normality is viewed as living in harmony with the seasons of life, and abnormality is viewed as disruption of the rhythm of life.

Ritual life of the African American church helps us visualize the influence of the African notion of rhythms of life. The significance of rituals related to birth, baptism, marriage, and funerals is notable. The point is that the life cycle perspective is a natural attraction to African American couples and families and can be used in understanding the problems they face. It is survival of the African tradition of life cycle transitions among African Americans that makes life cycle theory useful in conceptualizing therapeutic problems with this ethnic and racial group.

Poverty and racial discrimination have a disruptive influence on the life cycles of African Americans. Winston Gooden believes that "victimization because of race and class is inherently part of their stories."[6] The marginality and socioeconomic status influence how African Americans negotiate the tasks of life cycle; for example, race impacts the identity formation of African American youths. Romney Moseley discusses the "negative identity" that is foisted on them as the result of poverty, racism, narcotics, and unemployment.[7] The negative identity he talks about relates to Erik Erikson's belief that wider society only holds out limited roles for African Americans, which impact negatively their identity formation.[8]

Many African American men talk about the need for mentors for African Americans during adolescence and young adulthood. This means that they need models who can help them maintain integrity in their character while still being successful in preparing for adult roles in society. Billingsley in his book *Climbing Jacob's Ladder* talks about how those who are bicultural with their feet firmly planted in the African American family tradition find such models and values.[9] This rootedness in African American culture is one of the major reasons for the success of African American women in the work world, according to Algea Harrison.[10] The point is that racism offers significant challenges to African Americans becoming adult, but connections to African American family legacies are essential in making the transition from childhood to adulthood.

Racism and class status also impact African American marital life cycles; for example, in the clinical work of Arthur Jones it was found that African American couples often had dual commitments to the African American community and its values as well as to the middle-class images of employment success.[11] Such dual commitments, often referred to as double consciousness, made it difficult for husbands and wives to balance success and make marital cycle transitions. Marital couples who committed themselves to wider societal values of success had difficulty with intimacy and closeness needed to make it through the marital transitions.

Middle-Class African American Families

The major problem posed to middle-class African American families is their working in two worlds, the bicultural problem.[12] Some middle-class families are isolated from their extended-family roots and identify completely with the American mainstream. Others attempt to become bicultural by seeking to integrate the two and by living in two worlds. Such attempts, whether bicultural or complete acculturation, place added strains and stresses on the family making life cycle transitions. As in the case of Mr. P, he had no support group that could sustain him and help him maintain emotional and spiritual integrity in the midst of his job. He needed others to help him to see his work as a job and not as his whole life. His job-related fears prevented him from handling the tasks of midlife transition. Thus, environmental stressors can truly complicate the life cycle development and processes of the African American.

Because many middle-class African American families have aspired toward participation in wider culture, the dominant life cycle of wider culture seems to be very influential on them. That is to say, there is evidence that many middle-class black families pass through similar life cycle stages as do other middle-class families.[13] It is significant to note that many middle-class black families have adopted values that allow them to participate in the wider culture. These values, according to Billingsley, are stable kinship bonds, strong achievement orientation, positive parent-child relations, solid religious orientation, intellectual-cultural orientation, and strong work orientation.[14] These values are found in both single-parent families and two-parent families. In short, these values helped many middle-class black families to participate in the wider culture and negotiate similar life cycle transitions as other middle-class Americans. This does not mean, however, that poor African Americans do not undergo similar life cycle development as middle-class African Americans. However, the literature reveals that poor African American families have one additional environmental stressor that middle-class African American families can escape most of the time—poverty.

The Poor African American Family and the Life Cycle

There are many ways that the poor African American family life cycle differs from that of the middle-class African American family.[15] The differences relate to the culture of poverty, the structures of impoverished families, and characteristics of poor families.

The *culture of poverty* refers to the worldview shaping the behavior of poor families as they confront racism, tragedy, and suffering.[16] The culture of poverty is circular in that there are feedback forces in external society, namely, racism, helping to perpetuate chronic poverty. For example, equal choice exists for all Americans, but equal opportunity often does not exist for poor African Americans. There are many learned responses to the absence of opportunity and to a hostile environment as means of compensating for racism. Some of these responses are creative and adaptive. Others are maladaptive and perpetuate the condition. In addition, the training the poor require to obtain the skills needed to escape poverty is out of their reach. The supply of unskilled jobs is disappearing. All these factors contribute to a sense of hopelessness and low self-esteem. The end result is that many poor multiproblem families have a pervasive sense of impotence, rage, and despair.[17]

Poverty also seems to have a characteristic impact on the family life cycle. One can identify four characteristics that distinguish multiproblem African American families from middle-class African American families: (1) life cycles are often truncated in poor multiproblem African American families, (2) households are frequently female-headed and without extended-family ties, (3) numerous unpredictable life events bring stress on the families, and (4) there are no readily available resources to assist with the stressors, hence the need to rely on government and agency help to meet these unpredictable events.[18]

The poor multiproblem African American family also has severe problems doing appropriate life cycle tasks. Many males die just before or soon after retirement. Many of the elderly continue to work to make ends meet long after retirement age. No such thing as the empty-nest stage exists because elderly relatives tend to be active members in the expanding extended-family households with young children. Often three-generation families exist headed by a grandmother caring for her own children and grandchildren.

The point is that the life cycle theory is relevant to African Americans, although there needs to be modifications of it because of race and poverty.

A Comprehensive Model
of an African American Family Life Cycle

There are many different life cycles identified and explored within African American families.[19] This formulation has been very helpful to me in working with African Americans in pastoral counseling.

Formation:
Mating and Marriage

Mating and formation is a family stage and is characterized by two young adults differentiating from their families of origin and forming a new nuclear family of their own.[20] These two major processes of differentiating and forming a new relationship involve a great complexity of tasks and stresses in order to make the transition from singlehood to marriage. Two important tasks are revising the personal mythology that each spouse brings to the marriage and forming the couple or conjugal mythology on which to build a marriage.

Revising the personal mythology. Personal mythologies are self-convictions concerning how people feel about themselves, themselves in relationships with others, and the internalized ideals gathered from significant others. Personal myths are cognitive structures, and they are generated from families of origin.[21] They function to organize a person's experiences into a meaningful framework that informs everything the person does. A personal myth develops from a complex process, including: (1) reconstruction of experiences with family of origin and extended-family members in ways that become cognitive self-structures; (2) internalizing of roles, images, themes, and specific personality characteristics from significant others from the family of origin; (3) role taking based on significant exposure to literary characters encountered in reading and in the multimedia; and (4) cultural images that evolve from racism and discrimination.

With regard to the developmental cycle, the personal myth is formed and reformulated based on the developmental tasks that need to be accomplished at a specific transitional stage. The personal myth at a particular stage contains self-conviction themes, themes about ideal relationships with others, and ideal images of possible mates, of children and of family relationships, and racial and ethnic images within the socioeconomic, sociopolitical, and historical context.

At the mating and marriage stage one of the major tasks is differentiation of the self from the family of origin and extended family while retaining positive contact with them. The personal myth of each potential mate is related primarily to how well the young adult has or is achieving emotional connections with and self-differentiation from the family of origin and extended family. Self-differentiation assumes that persons who have achieved a good measure of self-differentiation have positive mythologies. These positive personal myths include themes related to positive self-esteem. Persons with positive myths see themselves able to enter into intimate relationships with others, capable to care for and value others, and able to form commitments with another person. They feel confident and have the capacity to enter into contractual arrangements with another; they regard themselves as able to share meanings and communicate clearly with another, and they have the skills to compromise and resolve interpersonal conflict.[22] Moreover, these people with positive myths are not overly vulnerable to the negative and stereotypical images imposed on them by wider society.

Persons who have not achieved a good enough level of self-differentiation have less positive personal mythologies. Their personal myths contain themes of low self-esteem, negative views of the self, and the lack of self-confidence in their abilities to form intimate relationships. They also develop contracts with others that are not mutual, but rather self- and other-destructive. The ability to share meanings and communicate clearly is impaired. Relationships are constantly conflicted without effecting a compromise. Such persons are vulnerable to negative images impressed on the racial and ethnic group members by wider society. In other words, the personal mythology is replete with themes that do not enable the person to participate fully in intimate relationships with others.

The specific content of the personal myths includes: (1) images of the ideal mate one wants, (2) the ideal child or children one wants, and (3) the ideal marriage and family images.[23] Personal myths also encompass self-images that the person has constructed as the result of a history of interaction within the family and encountering racial and ethnic images from wider society.

The specific developmental tasks during mating and marriage are to revise and rework the content of the personal mythologies in light of the actual mate that one has chosen. The personal myth becomes the norm for evaluating the potential mate and marital partner. The self-differentiated person will have the ability to revise his or her ideal mate image and change the content of the personal myth depending on the actual mate. However, those persons with less self-differentiation will seek to make the chosen mate conform to the ideal mate image through persuasion or coercion. Persons with low self-differentiation resist changes even when the developmental tasks needed for that behavior modification dictate change.

Forming the couple or conjugal mythology. The need to revise the personal myth based on the realities of the potential mate leads logically to the next family task in the mating and marriage stage. The second task of the mating and marriage family developmental task is to form the couple or conjugal mythology.

The coming together of two distinct personal mythologies forms the couple mythology.[24] *Couple mythology* is the beliefs and convictions that individuals bring to marriage concerning their ideal mate. It is a process that begins with mate selection and courtship, and involves actual attempts to marry someone who fits the ideal mate image. Ideal images involve images of the ideal spouse and images of the ideal marriage. These ideal images are both conscious and unconscious, and the more unconscious and subtle dimensions of the mate images come into play as the mating relationship continues.[25] These ideal images are formed based on experiences with members of the opposite sex, exposure to familial models of relating, and viewing other significant male and female relationships.[26]

The task of this stage is for the selected mate to revise his or her personal myths, ideal spouse, and ideal marriage images based on the reality of the other person and their new experiences together. Several options are open for accomplishing this task.[27] The first is to terminate the relationship if the potential mate does not meet the expected ideal. The second is to modify the personal and ideal mate image and accommodate it to the spouse-to-be. The third option is to attempt to bring about changes in the prospective spouse so that the person conforms more closely to the ideal mate image. In the latter case, strategies for conforming can vary from subtle coercion to outright physical punishment.

Depending on the degree of self-differentiation and connection one has achieved from the family of origin and extended family, mates can modify and accommodate their ideal images. The higher the self-differentiation, the better persons are able to engage in the mutual reshaping of the new couple mythology, based on their own experiences and revised images of each other. However, the lower the self-differentiation and the more conflict-laden the connection with the family of origin and extended family, the more difficult a time these persons will have in modifying their personal ideal spouse and ideal marriage mythologies.

Developing a mutual and shared new couple mythology marks the end of the mating and formation stage. The couple is ready for the next stage of transition. For those who decide to have children, this stage is called the *expansion stage*. For those who do not have children, this phase is called "the early years of the marriage."[28]

Expansion:
Parental Beginnings and Early Years

The expansion stage is marked by the addition of another person to the family. This stage becomes more complex because of the five types of life cycles it encompasses: the family life cycle, the marital life cycle, the adult individual life cycle of each adult, the child individual life cycle, and the cycles of each spouse's family of origin and extended family.[29] This phase involves at least three different generations or more when extended family is involved.

Among family tasks of this phase are (1) incorporating new family members, (2) facilitating individual growth and development of each family member, (3) maintaining the functional spousal relationship so that spousal satisfaction remains, (4) developing a parent-child subsystem for socialization of the child based on the child's developmental needs, (5) making room for extended-family members and relatives, especially grandparents, and (6) revising ideal child and ideal family mythologies.

The marital life cycle. This life cycle involves maintaining the spousal relationship and deepening the development of the couple mythology. The couple is developing commonly shared cherished stories and a history that can reflect that nurturance over the years. The *spousal subsystem* or relationship between husband and wife must be maintained as the primary subsystem of the family, and husband and wife need to deepen their mutuality and intimacy for the family to function.

The adult individual life cycle. The individual must continue the process of self-differentiation and connection with the family of origin and extended family. Also issues of vocation and work and balancing these concerns with home concerns become prominent. The individual's personal mythology needs to be continually in the process of revision so that it accommodates new experiences while maintaining continuity with the past.

The child individual life cycle. The child is totally dependent and has some very basic developmental needs. The child needs a safe and comfortable relational environment so that he or she can develop cognitive abilities, physical skills, interacting abilities, and ability to internalize social expectations. Moreover, the foundation is laid for the child's own personal mythology based on the quality of relationships existing with significant others.

The extended-family life cycle. This life cycle is characterized by family of origin members becoming grandparents, aunts, uncles, and dependent adults. The major task here is for the extended family to be connected to the parenting task without interfering with the parent-child subsystem of the family of creation. Relationships with the family of origin are crucial for the family of creation in order to continue developing its family mythology.

Revising the ideal child image. Each spouse brings into the marriage an ideal child and an ideal family image as part of his or her personal mythologies. A new personal mythology and a family mythology need to be created based on the realities of the new family and the actual child. A *family mythology* refers to ideal images of children and of a family that spouses as individuals bring to the marriage. Those who have achieved a good sense of self-differentiation and connection with the family of origin can do the task of revising the ideal child and ideal family mythologies. Those who have lower levels of self-differentiation and conflictive connectedness, however, have difficulty doing this revising task. It is essential that this re-visioning take place for the optimal growth and development of the child.

In addition to revising the family mythology is the family's need to lay an important basis for the child's eventual leaving and moving into the adult world. Crucial throughout the rearing of children are the values that enable African American children as well as youth to deal with wider society. Because of the history of racism in this country and its resurgence, it cannot be assumed that children will not encounter racial discrimination. Consequently, families must prepare their children and youth for this inevitability. Billingsley points out that this has been accomplished by African American families through the values they teach and the kinds of relationships they provide. These survival values and relationships include solid kinship bonds, achievement orientation, positive parent-child relationships, strong religious orientation, intellectual and cultural orientation, and a potent work orientation.[30] These values and relationships prepare the child for the tasks of the next stage of the life cycle and for meeting the demands of the adult world.

Contraction:
Individuation and Launching Stage

The next stage of the life cycle following childhood is the preparation of the adolescent and the young adult to depart from the home. This is called the *contraction stage.*[31] In this stage there are also family, marital, individual life cycle, and extended-family tasks. There are also crucial tasks related to the personal, marital, and family mythologies. While some are launched others may come into the home from the extended family.

The family life cycle developmental tasks embrace (1) releasing family members, (2) rearing adolescents, (3) letting children go, (4) dealing with the empty nest, (5) and incorporating new members by the marriage of the children as young adults as well as extended-family members.

Parents with adolescents. Part of the contraction stage is parenting adolescents. The basic task for the family during this phase is to prepare the adolescent for entrance into the world of adult responsibility and commitments.[32] There are also related tasks involving other levels of life cycles in the family and extended family: (1) parents and grandparents working through their unresolved conflicts (extended-family life cycle); (2) spouses beginning to renegotiate their marital contract and their personal, marital, and family mythologies (marital life cycle); and (3) parents working on their individual midlife crises (adult individual life cycle). There are also the individual adolescent life cycle tasks: (1) solidifying identity through autonomy and self-differentiation; (2) changing sexual roles and norms from those of parents; (3) becoming more responsible for decision making, and (4) establishing a personal mythology that will take the adolescent into young adulthood.

The family tasks in response to the adolescent involve redefining the family mythology by expanding it to encompass (1) developing flexible authority to permit increased independence; (2) parents becoming comfortable with their own sexuality to permit discussions with their adolescents; and (3) encouraging adolescents to participate in decision making while maintaining their parental executive authority. This latter point is crucial because adolescents do not need to be overwhelmed with premature responsibility, and the parents need to be aware of how to be supportive and encouraging while at the same time letting the authority go gradually as the adolescent becomes more mature.

Launching the young adult. Following the child's adolescence, the family must undertake the tasks associated with launching the young adult. The major family task for this period is continuing to let the young adult go, a process already initiated with the adolescent phase.

Marital tasks that must also be addressed include affirming the integrity of the marital relationship by revising the marital mythology. The marital relationship will take center stage again. The spouses must (1) rework the marital myth by expanding their marital narrative to include living with the empty nest, (2) deepen their intimacy despite declining physical abilities, and (3) resurrect the previous nurturing dimensions of their marital story or narrative.

Spouses also find themselves in the individual life cycle of middle adulthood. The major task here is to revise the personal mythology of each spouse to include (1) changing relationships with parents that might involve care for aging parents; (2) reevaluating aspirations, vocational and economic achievements; (3) laying a spiritual foundation that will sustain the person through declining physical health, retirement, and loss of loved ones; and (4) preparing to assume the role as stewards of the resources to make the world better for the next generation by intentionally attending to the family legacy of values.

Problems of discrimination and racism also have to be taken into consideration in this phase. Many African Americans hit the so-called glass ceiling beyond which they cannot go despite previous achievements. Others are concerned with developing their own businesses because of the racial climate. Others become preoccupied with making the racial climate better for the future.

The young adult also has individual life cycle tasks to accomplish, tasks that involve continued efforts to expand the personal mythology. These tasks entail (1) self-differentiating and connecting with the family of origin, (2) establishing self in career and vocational tracks, and (3) making choices of whether to marry or remain single.

The Postparental Years

Once the children leave home this phase begins. It ends when both parents have died.[33] The life cycle continues into the *postparental phase* where the adult children become parents, thereby making the aging parents grandparents and great-grandparents. The life cycles that are involved incorporate the marital life cycles of the aging parents and of their married children. The individual life cycles include the aging adults, the middle adult life cycle of their children, the young adult, adolescent, and child life cycles of grandchildren.

The family tasks during the postparental years consist of expanding the family mythology to include grandchildren and perhaps primary care for them, dealing with declining financial resources, and the need to change living arrangements, developing satisfying relationships with extended-family members, and moving into new roles as grandparents and as retired people. Another important task is to expand the family mythology to include in-laws.

The marital tasks of the postparental couple comprise revising the marital mythology to include supporting each spouse through declines and losses, recovering early marital memories and cherished history as a means of sustaining the marriage in the present, celebrating wedding anniversaries as extended-family events, making adjustments that are involved with retirement, and exploring the potential of in-law activities.

One aspect of the individual life cycle of the aging person is the task of revising the personal mythology to maintain a sense of personal and ego-integrity despite the aging process, possible illness, and eventual death. The aging person must begin to: deal with increasing dependency on previous generations, change social activities, adjust to changing physical abilities, cope with friends and family members dying, learn to deal with loneliness, and find one's place in life despite the aging process.[34]

In this chapter the emphasis has been on placing the problems and worldview that African Americans bring to counseling in a life cycle perspective. When this happens, the pastoral counselor has some significant handles for making interventions in these marriages and families. Significant in the exploration of the life cycle has been the focus on how personal, marital, and family myths had to be revised depending on the life cycle. In addition, social and cultural factors are present in the life cycles that the therapist should confront as well. The life cycle framework lends itself well to working with African American marriages and families in therapy.

Chapter Six

A Model
of Joining, Assessment,
and Intervention

The goal of this chapter is to develop a model of marital and family therapy that ties together the basic information that has been developed in the previous chapters. The areas to be explored include joining, assessing, and intervening in marriages and families. The key to this chapter is an integrative approach that draws from a variety of sources to serve the ends of liberated holistic growth of each marital partner and family member.

Some word needs to be said for the choice of the integrative approach as opposed to a more specific or exclusive intervention strategy. The rationale for using an integrative approach relates to the needs of those seeking pastoral counseling. Each person, couple, or family is unique. Their presenting problems are not the same, and their styles of interacting and personal dispositions are not uniform. Thus, it is better for the pastoral counselor to have the knowledge and skills to utilize different approaches to be flexible enough to respond to the divergent needs of the counselees.

Joining: The Client-Therapist Relationship
in Pastoral Counseling

Joining has to do with therapeutic intervention within a marriage or family and building a relationship. Boyd-Franklin emphasizes that African Americans are generally suspicious about the therapeutic process, and therefore, the initial contact with the family or marital partners is crucial.[1] She emphasizes that there must be a "gut level" joining with the couple or family almost from the beginning. This means that the therapist must give off the right vibes or communicate an openness to take seriously the concerns of the marriage or family without minimizing them.

The first thing I do when a person, couple, or family comes in is to attend to the presenting problem, but my concern is to connect with each person at a feeling level. I usually begin with the person who made the contact, and I ask him or her to tell me what concerns or what hurts. When the person expresses feelings I usually try to connect with the feeling immediately. In this way I hope to communicate the right vibes and create an environment of care.

A couple came to counseling where the presenting problem was initially financial. As the problem unfolded, the underlying difficulty was that the husband felt that he did not have the skills and knowledge to handle the money and that his wife did. He felt she ought to have the right to set the financial agenda, and she was resisting. They both bought into the religious idea that the man as head of the house meant being in charge and making all the decisions. She accepted this, but she also felt like a child in relationship to a parent.

Joining with this couple presented a problem because of the temptation to move in and challenge their ideas about what it meant to be the head of the house and the roles of males and females in the home. However, the key was to find a way of connecting to each spouse. Consequently, I began to explore each spouse's feelings. I explored with him how he felt about carrying the entire financial burden of the family. I explored with her how she felt about giving control of her money over to her husband. In joining the couple in this way, the issues began to be clarified, and the stage was set for them to decide how they wanted to handle their money as a couple. My goal was to connect with each spouse emotionally.

Boyd-Franklin also emphasizes that there is no such thing as an African American marriage or family. Rather, each marriage and family that the therapist encounters is unique with its own set of problems and concerns.[2] She emphasizes that one of the secrets of joining African American families comes as a result of allowing the family or marital partners to teach the therapist who they uniquely are. While acquaintance with African American culture is important, she stresses that such knowledge could be a stumbling block if used prematurely. The key is to connect emotionally with those who are present in the therapeutic session.

Finally, Boyd-Franklin emphasizes that credibility with African American marriages and families has to be earned.[3] This means that credentials and training are secondary to demonstrating openness to those who come for counseling. Attending to the feelings of each person and taking them seriously is a major way to gain credibility.

There is one exception to earning credibility, however. Pastoral counselors, whether African American or non-African American, seem to be trusted because of the role that religion plays in the lives of African Americans. Rather than being a drawback, African Americans seem to be more comfortable with clergy that have therapeutic skills. Therefore, joining may not be difficult. However, attending to feelings and demonstrating *empathy*—attempting to see the world through the eyes of the counselee—enhances credibility.

One explanation for the easy entry of clergy into the lives of African Americans is found in the research done by Thomas Pugh. He studied carefully the caregivers that African Americans turned to for help. He found that family members ranked high on the list followed by clergy. Professional caregivers were turned to after family members and clergy.[4] There may be less stigma going to pastoral counselors for help than there is for going to secular caregivers. That is, the African American community still feels that only crazy people need therapeutic help.[5]

The implication of this is that pastoral counselors, whether African American or not, have less difficulty initially joining with African American families. However, what needs to be done once potential counselees come for counseling? This question is explored next.

The writer's training was in Rogerian, existential, and Boston interpersonal perspectives that emphasized empathy and attending to the internal frame of reference and experience of the client as the major means of joining the family and marriage.[6] The writer draws on these emphases primarily because each marital partner, each family member, and each marriage and family is unique.

Ivan Boszormenyi-Nagy uses a concept called multidirectional partiality that helps me to transfer the concepts of empathy and attending to the internal frame of reference of clients into the arena of marital and family therapy.[7] *Multidirectional partiality* refers to the therapist's deep regard for the equitable investment in each family member and marital partner. This is accomplished by listening to each person and his or her complaints about the family and sequentially moving from one person to the next until all have been attended to. This approach requires the skills of empathy and genuine concern for each person and his or her way of seeing the family problem. Respect for each person's view of the problem and the family's way of understanding the problem is part of building a working therapeutic relationship as well.

Multidirectional partiality helps the pastoral counselor to join with each person and marriage or family. It facilitates the ability of the family members to teach the therapist who they are. This is essential for joining with African American families.

In summary, connecting with the family emotionally is essential in my view to intervening in the marital and family system. It is a prerequisite for making attempts to influence the marital and family system. Once the therapist has connected with each family member and the family system has been achieved, the process of therapy continues. The therapist-client relationship sets the stage for problem assessment, framing the problem, setting goals, and working toward goals. Without the initial therapist-client relationship therapy cannot proceed through its various stages.

The goal of connecting with each family member and marital partner is to help them reveal the presenting problem and the circumstances and history surrounding the problem. Connecting with them helps them to articulate how they understand their complaints. Once connecting takes place, the therapist can help move them to a broader understanding of the problem and to setting goals to attack the problem. When the therapy moves beyond the presenting problem and its history to the broader understanding of the problem (reframing in light of assessment of family process), the therapist knows that a therapeutic relationship has been formed.

The literature by black family therapists suggests that African American families are more likely to respond to therapeutic approaches that are problem-solving-oriented.[8] I have found this to be very true for many of the African American marriages and families with whom I have done pastoral counseling. Although there may be some serious underlying personal problems and family of origin difficulties underlying these problems, I have very little success in moving people toward dealing with the more personal issues related to the marital or family difficulties. I find that African American counselees stick with the presenting problem issues, and therapy is generally terminated when they feel that the presenting problem has been addressed successfully or not by pastoral counseling.

One example is illustrative. One African American couple came to pastoral counseling after being referred by their pastor. The pastor referred them to me because he realized that there were some very deep personal problems at work that were hindering the marriage. One such problem was that this was the third marriage of the husband. This was the wife's first marriage although she had a young child. The couple did all right together as long as they came to pastoral counseling.

Their presenting problem was that they could not communicate. Once I connected with each spouse emotionally, I gave them some things that they could do to improve their communication. For example, I helped the husband to put his frustrations into words rather than act them out with temper tantrums. I helped both of them to attend to what the other was saying and meaning. They were able to do this satisfactorily for a short period of time. However, there were underlying scripts that both inherited from their family of origin that made their relationship volatile. Yet they were not able to engage these issues. I tried individual sessions with both, but it seemed that each focused on the other as a result. Following about a three-week hiatus in our sessions, violence erupted, and they decided to seek divorce.

The point is that it is hard to move some African American families beyond the presenting problem focus and to deal with deeper interpersonal and personal dynamics. Those African American counselees who are more familiar with the therapeutic process and have some exposure to the therapeutic method can move toward deeper psychological dynamics in therapy.

The literature reports that African Americans will tend to respond to time-limited, problem-solving, child-focused, family therapy approaches.[9] Moreover, African Americans tend to need approaches to the therapeutic process that bring immediate changes.[10] I find this to be generally the case, although there are exceptions. This time-limited and problem-solving-oriented approach seems also suitable to the new emphasis on managed care where insurance companies pay only for short periods of therapy. I do take a lot of effort to focus on the presenting problem in the initial interview while I am employing multidirectional partiality. I think that the problem-solving, time-limited approaches to therapy must be the initial model to use with African Americans. However, this can be modified later depending on the needs of the marriage and family and their openness to explore other areas of their lives.

Emphasis on the presenting problem is often regarded as a strategic therapeutic approach employed by people like Jay Haley.[11] This approach emphasizes formulating the presenting problem and then designing an intervention strategy for resolving this problem.[12] John Patton reminds us that pastoral care and counseling are not problem solving; rather, they are hearing and remembering within relationships.[13] Consequently, the model utilized here is not just problem solving. Rather, it is an integrative model grounded in empathic and interpersonal relationships drawing on different theories and strategies for enhancing relationships. This approach uses strategic problem solving with African Americans once empathic joining of the family has taken place.

Assessment in Marital and Family Pastoral Counseling

In the early part of this book, emphasis on the worldview that African Americans bring to pastoral counseling was discussed. This worldview is religious, cross-generational, and extended-family-oriented, rhythmical in its life cycle, and narrative-oriented in terms of style of communication. Therefore, assessment of the problems that are brought to pastoral counseling needs to take very seriously this worldview. Moreover, the social context of racism and discrimination is reflected in the problems that African Americans bring to pastoral counseling. Consequently, it is possible to talk about theological and ethical, contextual, cross-generational, and life cycle assessments. These varied factors will be systematically presented through a comprehensive view of assessment.

The critical issue in assessment for African Americans focuses on the presenting problem. Consequently, the assessment begins with exploring those factors that impact the problem that is presented by couples and families.

Theological and Ethical Assessment

Religious and theological assessment involves examining the presenting problem in light of the worldview that marriage partners and family members bring to pastoral counseling. Moreover, this worldview needs to be assessed based on the norm of liberated holistic growth and the ethic of love. Significant here is the ability to operationalize the definitions that help pastoral counselors to assess the worldview of African American counselees.

When the presenting problem is being explored, it is important to attend to the religious factors related to the presenting problem. For example, an African American couple came for pastoral counseling. Their presenting problem was that they were having marital conflict and were threatening to split up because the hostility was so great. As the problem surfaced, it appeared that the husband moved to a new job while the wife was trying to complete her basic college degree. The husband had finished his degree, but the wife had not. He was making decisions based on his positioning himself for promotion. He didn't take her feelings into consideration at all.

The wife got pregnant and felt that her goal of finishing college was threatened. She would be the first person to finish college in her extended family, and this was very important to her. Therefore, she was depressed and angry, because she could not finish her education. The concern about finishing college, the recent move, her husband's insensitivity to her plight, and becoming a parent for the first time were multiple factors in their marital conflict.

The religious factor surfaced with regard to the role of the dutiful wife. She had been taught that a good Christian woman who loved her husband followed him wherever he went. He also believed this and took this for granted. He could not understand why she would complain about basic Christian beliefs.

The religious worldview surfaced as the presenting problem. The pastoral counselor can ask counselees if there are religious dimensions related to the problem. This should be routine with African American counselees early in the counseling relationship.

Investigating the influence of religious values on the presenting problem in marital and family life involves the following questions: (1) What religious values inform the ideal image of marital and family life? (2) What religious values are drawn on for understanding the role of males and females in the marriage and family? (3) What religious rules govern who makes decisions in the marriage and family? (4) What religious rules exist concerning the growth and development of each family member? What images of God exist in the marriage and family, and how do these images operate in the marriage and the family? (5) Are there religious values that support patriarchy? (6) Are the religious values sexist? (7) What impact do these various religious values have on marital and family functioning?

Contextual Assessment:
Marital and Family Stressors

This section seeks to explore assessment of the social context surrounding the presenting problem. The concept of external stressors is utilized.

External Stressors

Bicultural challenges, racial and economic pressures that impact the marriage and family are external stressors. To make these concepts operational the basic questions are the following: (1) Is the presenting problem related to living between two cultures? (2) What job-related pressures are involved in the presenting problem, and are these pressures related to job discrimination? (3) Is the presenting problem related to pressures for advancing in the job, and what impact does this have on commitment to family values?

One illustration of these factors is that Mr. P was preoccupied with not being poor. He overidentified with his job and what it took to be successful. This was his major concern, and he expected his wife and family to understand this. He also demanded their full loyalty and unquestioned support. He felt he was entitled to this given how the black man had been treated in the United States. This expectation was not only unrealistic; it put too much pressure on Mrs. P to ignore her needs. She felt she could only take responsibility for her own life and those of her children. She felt her husband must pull his own weight.

The influence of racial oppression on the presenting problems that African Americans bring can be put into assessment language. (1) Are there pressures on marital partners and family members related to racial discrimination on the job? (2) How does the marital partner or family member describe these discriminatory pressures? (3) How is the marital partner or family member handling these pressures? (4) How is the family or family member responding to these pressures?

One key factor in African American marital and family concerns is the relationship of racial oppression and the manhood issues of African American men. One response of African American men to racism is compulsive masculinity. Here *compulsive masculinity* refers to males adopting norms of toughness, emotional detachment, sexual conquest, manipulation, and thrill seeking as a response to economic marginality and racial discrimination.[14] In compulsive masculinity the worldview is present-oriented and attaches no value to work, sacrifice, self-improvement, or service to family, friends, or community.[15] The compulsive masculinity factor plays a significant role in many of the problems that I encounter working with African American couples and families. Often, protecting the African American male ego is a major component that cannot be ignored when doing pastoral counseling with African American males and females.[16]

While African American men respond to racism with compulsive masculinity, a characteristic response of an African American woman to racism is the internalization of self-hatred. This is manifested through allowing herself to be blamed by society and black men for the ills of the African American community. She extends herself for the concerns of the community at the expense of herself. She is often an overfunctioner taking on more than her share of the workload in families, and she uses a variety of self-destructive means to hold on to her man, including taking on more of the financial burden. This is internalized racism, because she takes problems on that she neither created nor can solve.[17]

Vertical Stressors

In addition to external pressures on the family, there are stressors within the family. The first such stressor has to do with *vertical stressors*, or patterns in the marriage and family that are passed on from generation to generation. These stressors include family patterns, family legacies, family myths, and family secrets. The basic question is, How is the presenting problem of African Americans related to vertical stressors?

Certain family problems are multigenerational. One such example is an African American female who is raising her two teenage children alone. She came to pastoral counseling initially because she felt inadequate as a parent. She had just discovered that her daughter had been molested by a family member, and she felt powerless to do anything about it. She resolved that she was going to confront this problem by exposing the family member and drawing in the authorities. When she attempted to do this, the wife of the perpetrator defended him, and the other family members ignored my counselee. When this happened, she was devastated, and she began to explore the history of how her extended family responded to the abuse of females.

She discovered a multigenerational pattern of abuse going back to her grandmother. She also found that there was some religious fatalism handed down by the females to their daughters that helped to perpetuate the abuse. Her grandmother and mother, who both had been sexually molested, felt that nothing could be done. They felt that this was their fate. They believed that God would find a way to deal with this; however, God's way for them was to keep it quiet.

My counselee had been abused also and kept it quiet. She decided that she would no longer be silent, and decided to break the pattern. After about a year of pastoral counseling she took on the family secret. She was less then satisfied with the results. Many families react to whistle-blowers negatively. My counselee said that perhaps the other women in the extended family will watch closely their husbands and brothers because of her courage.

Although sexual abuse and other forms of abuse against African American women are not unique, the influence of religion on African American people is very strong. Many African American women turn to religion to help deal with their victimization, and some do it in ways that exacerbate the victimization. For example, I have one counselee who believes that she is the biblical character of Eve. She believes that she deserves to be abused and that God is punishing her for the sins she committed in her past. Therefore, she tolerates verbal abuse from her ex-husband. Fortunately, she does not tolerate physical abuse. Her belief that she is Eve is not easily overcome therapeutically, and she only began to explore its influence after a year of individual pastoral counseling.

The taking of her husband's abuse and allowing herself to be blamed for his problems is an example of the internalization of racism. While there is family legacy from the family of origin, she feels responsible for this man's life and solving his problems. This is a common pattern that reflects accepting the blame for the problems that black males face.

The vertical stressors in the family that are related to the presenting problem are not always obvious in the beginning. However, there are questions that could be asked initially to probe the sensitive area of family myths, secrets, and legacies. These questions involve how marital partners and family members are related to their previous generations. The basic question is, Does the presenting problem have a cross-generational history? This can be found out by doing a *genogram*, or a cross-generational history.

When one does genograms to uncover cross-generational material, it is important to heed the warning of Boyd-Franklin, who points out that *genogram exploration*, or developing a design of the family's generational history, needs to be done carefully.[18] What she means is that genograms need to be constructed following the joining with families and not prior to this. Seeking historical information is often viewed as prying into family business by many African American families.[19]

Horizontal Stressors

Following the assessment of the vertical stressors comes an assessment of the *horizontal stressors*, or the developmental and nodal transitions that people confront. These transitions include individual, marital, and family life cycles. Horizontal stressors also include obstacles that people confront that challenge customary problem-solving methods that people utilize to adjust. Nodal events are associated with divorce, retirement, and geographical relocation and losses and threats of losses. The basic question for assessing horizontal stressors is, What are the life cycle transitions, situational crises (losses and threats of loss), and nodal events (divorce, retirement, relocation) that the family or marriage is facing?

Every presenting problem can be put into a life cycle perspective. This needs to be done routinely when doing counseling with African Americans. What makes this unique for African Americans relates to unresolved problems of ego-identity. This was certainly the case with Mr. P, who constantly had problems of personal inadequacy related to being black in a white system. He never developed a quiet confidence that he fit or belonged. He constantly feared being a failure, inadequate, inferior. He also feared that whites would criticize his work. This reflects the fact that he had difficulty finding a comfortable fit between his self-understanding and the appropriate cultural affirmation of that understanding. This represents a problem of identity formation where one's self-understanding is confirmed by culture through an appropriate job.

Because ego-identity is related to becoming an adult, difficulty in forming an ego-identity impacts the adult stages of development. This means that there are problems with developing adult roles and accomplishing the tasks related to adult transitions; for example, as one grows older and goes through the stages of individual, marital, and family life, difficulties arise. Each life cycle transition calls for people to be flexible and to take multiple roles in a variety of settings. However, people who have difficulty in identity formation find themselves locked into certain roles incapable of changing roles to meet the demands of adulthood. Mr. P, for example, spent most of his time trying to fulfill roles related to the marketplace and neglecting the roles related to family life and personal development.

Putting the presenting problem in a life cycle perspective also relates to the concept of cluster stress. Here the emphasis is on the presence of multiple stressors at a given time in the family or marriage. One of the results of racism and discrimination is the fact that African American individuals, marriages, and families face multiple stressors. This means that they often face two or more stressors at one time. For example, Mr. and Mrs. P were in different stages of the midlife crisis; they were raising a preadolescent and a small child; he faced the constant threat of unemployment because of racism; and both Mr. and Mrs. P were laboring under the weight of difficult family legacies.

The point is that a pastoral counselor with African Americans needs to assess the presence of multiple stressors impacting the lives of African Americans. Paying attention to such stressors can help the pastoral counselor attend to the most salient problem that the marriage or family is facing. The pastoral counselor can help the family put the presenting problem in its proper framework so that they can envisage what is happening to them.

The major difficulty I have with addressing the multiple stressors that African Americans face is the problem of perpetuating the victim mentality. Helping African Americans understand their problems in light of racism and discrimination might contribute to feelings of helplessness and inadequacy. The critical problem for the pastoral counselor is to help African Americans face the reality of racism and discrimination without thinking of themselves as helpless victims. This means that the pastoral counselor needs to help the African American people to define the presenting problem in ways that take racism and discrimination seriously while pointing to directions that can be taken to deal with the presenting problem. The pastoral counselor's task is to help the marital partners and family members to address the areas of the problem over which they have the most control.

For example, there was a couple whose presenting problem was the husband's anger that he exhibited toward his wife and family members. It turned out that his anger erupted because of job-related stress. He was working with a difficult manager who he felt related to him in very negative ways. He felt that the manager was motivated by racism. Therefore, my task was to help the husband (1) to do reality testing with regard to the behavior of his boss; (2) to identify when his anger was developing and to be clear about its source; (3) to find ways to communicate to family members what was going on; (4) to find ways to talk about what he was feeling with management without jeopardizing his job; (5) to explore ways that he could get himself out from under the manager if it became too unbearable.

The crucial pastoral counseling skills needed are to help the counselee to assume responsibility for the problem without him or her being overwhelmed. Victimization needs to be taken seriously, but the pastoral counselor must help the counselee address those aspects of the problem over which he or she has control. In summary, it is important to acknowledge the feelings of victimization, and to help persons address those solvable dimensions of the problem.

Assessing Marital Conflict

When marital partners are presenting their problems to the pastoral counselor, the pastoral counselor needs to assess the marital environment.[20] What is the emotional climate like? Is the atmosphere safe and warm? Is it calm or turbulent and unsafe? Is there presence of active marital conflict?

The presenting problem also deals with communication and activity time together as a couple. The questions in assessing communication focus on types of communication and components of communication. What is the degree of openness of communication around difficult issues? Is there free self-disclosure in the exchange of communication? Is the verbal communication critical, undermining, and disaffirming or is it supportive, affirming, and affectionate? Is there a balance between affection, praise, and criticism? Do spouses trust the truth of the other's communication (credibility)? With regard to activity together, is there shared activity and is there time spent working toward meeting each other's heart hungers or emotional needs?

Another area of marital assessment related to the presenting problem concerns how the marital partners make connections with each other during the conflict. What is the balance in the couple between emotional connection and distancing? Does one spouse understand the space boundary issues of the other? Is there intrusion into the other's space or is there moving away as an attempt to get more space? Has the couple worked out a way to respect personal boundary needs as well as to meet the need for connecting?

How do spouses assume responsibility for themselves while also sharing responsibility mutually with regard to the presenting problem? The major question in regard to mutual functioning is, Does one spouse overfunction and the other underfunction? The basic issue is, How do spouses function as individuals in performing parenting, household chores, and economic tasks?

Major presenting problems in marriage often center around sex, money, parenting, and in-laws. The major themes running through these issues are power and control. Power and control have to do with feelings of personal adequacy and competence. The lower the level of personal adequacy, the higher the need to control and have power through overt or covert means. Therefore, the critical question is, How do marital partners deal with the issues of power and control as they deal with the presenting problem? Are sex, money, in-laws, and parenting areas where control and power are exercised in positive or negative ways? How is power and control used to facilitate or hinder the growth of marital partners?

These three concerns of money, power, and sex take on added meaning for African Americans when racism and racial discrimination are factors. For example, I have counseled with African American men who have had difficulty functioning sexually because of medical problems. This took on added meaning for them given the nature of the forced emasculation of black men that exists in wider society. I often give credit to both husband and wife when they come with this concern, because it would be so easy for the male to refuse to come for counseling. The wife is generally encouraging and understanding when the male comes for counseling.

Another area of assessment relates to marital paradigms. *Marital paradigms* are guiding images or reference models that influence the couple's relationship.[21] For example, is the image surrounding the presenting problem closed and traditional? In this model the roles tend to be hierarchical, decisions relate to tradition, and conformity is valued. Second, are the images random and individualistic? In this second model each marital partner's needs come before the relationship. Or is the image open and verbal? In this model a positive tension exists between individual and relationship needs. For example, is there flexibility in roles; is there consensus building through communication and negotiation, and is leadership rooted in mutual collaboration and joint solution?

The concern for marital images and models for African Americans is crucial. Often, African Americans come to pastoral counseling with closed and traditional images of marriage. Consequently, the presenting problem is often framed with this understanding. Pastoral counselors need to be aware of this.

Triangles are important in marital assessment of the presenting problem of African Americans. Because of the emphasis on extended families among many African Americans, the potential always exists for drawing others into the marital conflict. When there is marital pain, sometimes the conflict can be held within the marriage partners and does not spill over into other relationships. However, if the marital pain cannot be held within the marital dyad, third parties may be drawn into the marital conflict to ease the pain. The process of drawing third parties into the marital pain for the purposes of easing the pain is called *triangulation.*[22] It is characteristic for one spouse to disconnect with the conflictual spouse and connect with a third party. This connecting can be with a child, multigenerational family members, external persons through extramarital affairs, or social networks. The purpose of the triangulation is to take pressure off the marital conflict.

The basic question for assessing the presence of conflict asks, Is the marital conflict contained within the marital dyad? If not, who is drawn into the marital dyad to relieve the pressure?

In assessing marital conflict, the pastoral counselor must ask the ultimate question whether the marriage contributes to the liberated holistic growth of each marital partner. Does the marriage and its dynamics create a safe space for the self-differentiated growth of each marital partner? Is there a good balance between attending to the growth needs of each partner? Such questions help to assess whether the marriage is functioning for both partners rather than for just one.

Assessing the Family

In the assessment of marital conflict surrounding the presenting problem, the emphasis is on the marital dyad. In the assessment of family conflict, the emphasis shifts away from the dyad and the focus is on the entire family. For African Americans, Boyd-Franklin lifts up several areas of assessment: boundaries, alignment, power, differentiation, the family projection process, and the multigenerational transmission process.[23] When assessing these areas in families, the pastoral counselor needs to visualize how these dynamics impact the presenting problem.

Boyd-Franklin says that boundary issues are complex for African American families.[24] *Boundaries* define who participates in the family and how. Normal functioning African American families generally have very close relationships. Sometimes the lines separating roles and functioning get blurred. This happens cross-generationally where the roles between parents and grandparents get cloudy. This permits the children to play one generation off against the other generation when it is not clear who is really in charge in the family. In my practice I see grandparents taking away the primary parenting responsibility from the parent, and I have also seen parents abdicating their role so that grandparents can take over the parenting function. The critical problem is when the boundaries are not clear enough to facilitate adequate parenting.

Sometimes the boundaries are too clear and rigid. This means that the lines separating family members are rigid permitting no real family interaction.[25] This often means being cut off from extended-family relationships. Because extended-family relationships tend to be important to African Americans the cutoffs and disengagements in these families need careful attention in pastoral counseling.

Because of the extended-family nature of African American families, there are alliances and coalitions. *Alliances* are cooperative working relationships where families work toward common ends. *Coalitions* are several family members working against other family members. Alliances and coalitions need to be attended carefully to ascertain their relationship to the presenting problem. This is especially the case when coalitions are cross-generational and dysfunctional.

The issue of power is also problematic in African American extended families. *Power* has to do with decision making and its ability to affect the family's life. This is crucial when the power to make decisions rests in extended-family members' hands; for example, I have seen some families in therapy where the power was in the grandparents' hands and this did not become apparent immediately in therapy.

Problems with regard to self-differentiation also appear in African American families. Self-differentiation has to do with a sense of self apart from others. The crucial issue in assessing the presenting problem is related to balancing the relationship between self-differentiation and commitment to the extended family. This is a problem in extended families where there are close relationships. The following question could be used to assess problems related to differentiation. Does the family have the requisite skills for balancing individual needs and family needs, and for balancing the need for self-differentiation and family togetherness?

The *family projection process* relates to a particular child being designated by the family as "the problem."[26] In African American families this projection process of designating the problem person often relates to secrets about birth, the paternity of the child, and skin color differences. These factors are key when a particular child is presented as the problem.

The *multigenerational transmission process* is the family projection process transmitted from one generation to the next over several generations.[27] This can be seen in the earlier case of the sexual abuse of the granddaughter, mother, and grandmother. This happened basically because of the silence that was taught generation after generation. The point is that presenting problems may be the result of the multigenerational projection process. Careful attention needs to be paid to putting the presenting problem into its cross-generational context.

The point of assessment is to determine how to help the family or marriage deal effectively with the presenting problem. Goals need to be set and intervention strategies designed for dealing with the presenting problem.

Marital and Family Intervention

The Goals of Therapy

Once the joining process has taken place and the presenting problem is explored in its broadest possible context, therapy moves to the goal-setting stage. Goal setting is a joint effort between the therapist and the marriage partners and family members. The counselees present their chief complaint or problem. As the pastoral counselor listens to the problem and explores its history (including its generational nature) he or she formulates some hypotheses about the dynamics and processes at work in the family. When the therapist gets a grasp of the problem and its current context, he or she may want to take the marital partners and the family through a genogram exploration so that the therapist can see the connection between the current problem and past history. Once this is done, observations need to be shared with marital partners and the family in nontechnical language. This is followed by asking family members and marital partners to state precisely what each would like to see happen in the marriage and family as a result of the informational input from the therapist.

Goal setting is a joint venture. The therapist makes input but respects the family's right to set the goals in collaboration with the therapist. The therapist can share his or her own goals for the family to see if they too can be part of the process. However, the therapist should respect the family's goals without imposing his or her goals on the family. Moreover, the therapist needs to get informed consent about how therapy will proceed.

Goals along with the presenting problem should be the focus of each session. Keeping the presenting problem and the stated goals in focus helps to chart the progress and movement toward achieving the goals. The goals should be specific enough and stated in operational terms to be able to be charted in each session. For example, a couple comes for pastoral counseling related to problems of an impending separation resulting from the husband's job. He was having to leave his family for a year in order to fulfill some job responsibilities. They wanted to work through some very strong feelings they were confronting because of this situation. Therefore, every issue that surfaced was therapeutically related to their presenting problem related to the feelings of separation.

The length of therapy depends on the nature of the goals that have been set. Behavioral and action goals for improving communication and changing transactional patterns can involve brief therapy from five to twelve sessions. Self-differentiation goals and goals of changing ideal images of the mate, child, and family take longer. This could involve six months to several years. Dealing with multigenerational patterns of interaction also require longer periods of time. It must be kept in mind that African Americans generally prefer shorter forms of therapy and problem-solving approaches.

The Therapy Process

Once the client-therapist relationship has been established and the goals have been set, the process of accomplishing the goals can begin. I understand the process of accomplishing goals is to take place in phases.[28] The first phase of therapy involves establishing the therapist-client relationship, broadening the understanding of the presenting problem, and setting goals. The next phase of therapy is the middle phase where the family and the therapist move toward accomplishing the goals. This phase is often characterized by the family holding on to its existing family interaction and homeostatic balance despite its stated goals. The role of the therapist is to help the family move beyond its present homeostatic balance toward its stated goals. How the therapist does this depends on his or her preferred mode of treatment.

My own style of helping marital partners and family members move toward their stated goals and introducing change in the family include (1) coaching (meeting periodically to plan the ways individuals approach members of their family of origin) individuals as they seek to self-differentiate themselves from the family of origin, (2) bringing in other family members (parents, relatives, and siblings) to stimulate change, (3) using the marital and family-therapist interaction as a source of feedback to introduce change into the marriage family, (4) using my own feelings, reactions to and experience of the marriage or family as a way to introduce change in the marriage system and family system (self-disclosure), (5) commenting on transactional patterns and making connections between present marital and family behavior and past generations to introduce change, (6) teaching specific tasks, (7) giving homework assignments, and (8) siding with particular marital partners and family members.

I take full responsibility for the methods used to introduce change, and I also take responsibility for creating a safe environment where the marriage or family can move at its own pace toward accomplishing its goals. My function is to help the family be aware of how it is moving toward its stated goals, how it seeks to maintain frustrating existing patterns, and to help the family monitor progress toward its goals. Termination comes when the therapist and clients explore goal achievement or when the marriage or family and therapist agree that they do not want the changes it once preferred. Cutting therapy short comes when the marriage or family prefers its current patterns over the goals that have been set. Often married couples or families will not return when this happens. The best scenario, however, is when the therapist interprets the marriage or family's preference for existing patterns of interaction and an agreement is made that they would return when they were ready to move toward the stated goals. Optimally, termination comes when the goals have been accomplished to the satisfaction of the family and the therapist. Termination should only proceed when the goals have been explored with the family, and the therapist and family have mutually agreed that therapy should be terminated. However, other goals can be established so that therapy can continue. This also is decided mutually between therapist and family.

In summary, the process of pastoral counseling with African American marriages and families begins with the first contact between therapist and client and proceeds through three distinct phases. Phase I is establishing client-therapist relationship, exploring the presenting problem, putting the presenting problem in a broader context, and setting goals. Phase II involves the family moving toward its stated goals with the help of the therapist. Phase III is the termination period where the goals have been accomplished and there is mutual agreement that the therapy is over.

Chapter Seven

Sexual Dysfunction in Marriage

Sexual dysfunction involves the failure of one or both partners to be able to complete the act of genital sex. Often in males, the problem is the inability of the male to have and maintain an erection. In females the problem can relate to the inability to achieve an orgasm. Many other problems are associated with the ability to function sexually in a genital way, but the inability to achieve an erection and to have an orgasm are the most common.

Sexual dysfunction among African American couples presents many concerns because of the linking of sex and white racism in the history of the United States. The racial stereotypes are that African Americans are sexually overactive and derive more pleasure than other races from sex. African American men are viewed with extra sexual prowess and African American women are viewed as sexually more desirable in the racial stereotypes.

In the context of racial stereotypes about sex is the response of African Americans to their own sexuality.[1] African American couples desire sexual pleasure and satisfaction just like any normal couple. However, when this fails, the self-esteem of those involved is impacted, and the racial stereotypes come into play, especially for African American men. Because of the values associated with compulsive masculinity, which is often a compensation for failure to fulfill the traditional images of manhood, African American men respond to their own sexual dysfunction with great concern. Sexual dysfunction not only conjures up fears of being sexually impotent but it becomes symbolic of the plight of African Americans in wider society.

African American women also have concerns about their own self-esteem if they are not able to enjoy sex through achieving orgasm.[2] While African American women are concerned about sexual dysfunction in themselves, racial and sexual stereotypes of themselves held by wider society seem to be less important for them than are other concerns. In general, African American women's self-esteem seems to be more invested in procreation and rearing children than in their ability to perform the sex act. Many refuse to fall prey to the sexual racist stereotypes of others.[3] Moreover, many African American women seem to derive pleasure from making sure that their "man" is happy sexually given the proper relational atmosphere of concern and love. The concern for rearing children and pleasing their man are both related to the traditional images of the role of females held by many African American women. In male compulsive masculinity, however, compensatory responses to the failure of manhood put more emphasis on the sex act itself.

This chapter will focus on the problem of sexual dysfunction. Ideas related to compulsive masculinity play a significant role in the sexual dysfunctional problem. Moreover, the model developed in the last chapter will be employed to give shape to this chapter.

To this end the case of Mr. and Mrs. P will be the focus. Mr. and Mrs. P were introduced in chapter 3. The summary of the case would be helpful to open the discussion on sexual dysfunction.

Summary of the Case
of Mr. and Mrs. P

Mr. P sought marital pastoral counseling because he wanted more emotional and sexual intimacy with his wife, Mrs. P. When they came for counseling it was apparent that Mr. P had marital goals, and Mrs. P had more personal goals. She wanted to grow and develop while he wanted her to sacrifice her growth for the sake of the marriage.

Mr. P is forty-five years of age and employed in the corporate world. Mrs. P is thirty-seven and works in a local industrial park. She is unhappy because she had to sacrifice her career and professional goals so that he could pursue his goals.

They have two children. Both are boys ages three and twelve. He had been married previously and has one child from his first marriage.

They brought to their marriage poor relationships with their families of origin and many resentments about being forced to be caretakers of their younger brothers and sisters. They were unhappy about losing their childhoods, and this has impacted the ways they conduct themselves in their marriage.

Mr. P has problems with impotency and is very frustrated that his wife is not more concerned about this problem. She finds his sexual inadequacy convenient so that she can put all her effort into pursuing her personal growth goals. He gets frustrated because of her pursuit of personal goals and tries to use traditional religion to coerce her into performing traditional marital goals.

A brief summary of the model would be helpful at this time. Following this I will explore in detail how I employed each step of the model with this particular case.

A Model of Joining, Assessment, and Intervention

Joining
    1. Multidirectional Partiality
    2. Attending to Presenting Problem

Assessment
    1. External Stressors
        a. Bicultural challenges
        b. Racial and economic pressures
        c. Religious values
    2. Vertical Stressors
        a. Family patterns
        b. Family legacies
        c. Family myths
        d. Family secrets
        e. Concepts
            (1) emotional cutoffs
            (2) self-differentiation
            (3) multigenerational transmission
    3. Horizontal Stressors
        a. Developmental life cycle transitions
            (1) individual
            (2) marital
            (3) multigenerational family
        b. Situational crises
            (1) losses
            (2) threats of loss
        c. Nodal events
            (1) divorce and remarriage
            (2) retirement
            (3) geographical relocation
        d. Cluster stress

Marital Assessment
    1. Emotional Climate
        a. Safety
        b. Temperature
        c. Turbulence
    2. Maintaining Marital Relationship
        a. Communication
            (1) around toxic issues
            (2) free self-disclosure

        (3) supportive affirmation
        (4) credibility
    b. Shared activity
3. Marital Fusion
    a. Emotional connection
    b. Emotional distancing
    c. Reciprocal functioning
        (1) overfunctioning
        (2) underfunctioning
4. Major Conflicts
    a. Sex
    b. Parenting
    c. In-laws
5. Marital Paradigms
    a. Closed/traditional
    b. Random/individualistic
    c. Open/verbal
    d. Synchronous/serene
6. Marital Mythology
    a. Ideal spouse image
    b. Ideal marriage image
7. Triangles
8. Theological Assessment
    a. Growth facilitating
    b. Growth inhibiting

Family Assessment
1. Boundaries
    a. Between individuals
    b. Between generations
    c. Between subsystems
2. Contextual Clarity
    a. Direction of communication
    b. Role definitions-parental coalition
3. Leadership
    a. Egalitarian
    b. Power struggles
    c. Authority and responsibility
4. Autonomy
    a. Encouraging autonomy
    b. Encouraging self-differentiation
5. Comfort in Relating
    a. Presence of empathy

6. Negotiation
    a. Clear communication
    b. Conflicts addressed
7. Capacity to Accept Change
8. Family Mythology
    a. Ideal child image
    b. Ideal family image
9. Theological Assessment
    a. Growth facilitation
    b. Growth inhibition

Marital and Family Intervention
1. Goals of Therapy
2. The Therapy Process
    a. Early phases
    b. Middle phases
    c. Termination

Joining

Mr. P contacted me by phone for pastoral counseling after his pastor referred him to me. I took the opportunity to explore with him, in a general way, the nature of the problem as he saw it. When he and his wife came for pastoral counseling, I asked him to reiterate what he had said on the phone so that the first session could commence. In having Mr. P reiterate what he had said on the phone, I was seeking to make a connection with him and his way of seeing the problem and the world. This did not mean that I was not interested in Mrs. P's way of viewing the world. If she had been the one to make the first contact, I would have begun the first session by asking her to give a summary of what was said in our initial phone contact. As it turned out, Mr. P's major motivation for contacting me first was to make sure that he influenced how I saw the problem from his vantage point. He had a great deal of anxiety about how I, as an African American man, might view him as an impotent male.

The concept of multidirectional partiality helps me to conceptualize what I do in the earliest stages of pastoral counseling. I began with Mr. P and how he saw the presenting problem. However, I knew that eventually I would get to Mrs. P and her conception of the problem. While Mr. P could have felt good about my starting first with him, this was a short-lived feeling. Eventually, his anxiety about his manhood emerged as I tried to engage Mrs. P.

Mr. P began by complaining about his wife's lack of emotional intimacy and sexual response to him. I felt that he was embarrassed by his sexual impotency, and I felt he wanted to make sure that he put his interpretive spin on it because of his anxiety about his manhood. I accepted his spin initially, because my concern was to foster a relationship so that the presenting problem could emerge. Second, I did not want my response to what he was revealing about himself to scare him away from the pastoral counseling process. However, I did not focus on his complaints about his wife. What I did was to keep the focus on him by asking him to comment on how he felt about being unable to function sexually.

Because of his uneasiness about how I saw him as a male, I paid very close attention to his consternation and tried to help him to feel comfortable in my presence. I expressed how difficult it must be for him to have to talk with me about such a difficult subject as impotency.

Mrs. P was not concerned about the sexual impotency of her husband at all. She did not view the problem as his inability to function sexually. Rather, she welcomed her husband's impotency. She felt that this gave her the time to deal with her major complaint about the marriage. Her major complaint was that she felt deceived and disenchanted because he did not deliver on his promises to provide materially for her and her two children. She felt that he had character flaws, and she felt stupid for believing that he could provide the kind of financial resources they needed without her income. Her major anger was that she had given up a perfectly good job, a home, and her extended family to follow him as he chased his career dreams.

Both Mrs. P and Mr. P had very traditional images of marriage. They both believed in the traditional roles of males and females. If the financial resources had been there, the crises would not have emerged. She felt she could work with his sexaul impotency if there had not been problems in the financial areas.

Mrs. P was angry because she realized that she had given up her life and her personhood to be married. She also was realizing that the meeting of the traditional ideal of marriage and family was not going to work. She began to see that she had to develop her own life and career if she hoped to have some semblance of happiness. Mr. P, however, felt that he would be able to deliver financially and that the debt he had accumulated because of the pursuit of his economic dreams was only temporary. Even though there was adequate money to be comfortable, Mr. P had created a great deal of debt pursuing his self-image as a successful businessperson. Mrs. P realized that this self-image was deeply ingrained in Mr. P, and she felt he could not change.

What surfaced as the presenting problem initially was only one symptom among many. What the presenting problem appeared to be, in my mind, was that both had the same ideal image about what marriage and family life would be according to the traditional model. Mr. P also had an ideal self-image that made him extend himself financially in ways that kept the family living from hand to mouth. Mrs. P realized this and responded with anger toward her husband. Later on in the session, she articulated that she realized that what was necessary was revising the ideal marriage image so that they could be more realistic. Mr. P, however, did not agree. He fully expected a big financial bonus to come, and when it did, he felt that they could reach the ideal. Consequently, the problem turned out to be a marital mythology where initial expectations about marriage had to be reworked based on the reality of the financial situation.

Complicating Mr. P's ideal marriage image was his own self-image as a male. Because feelings about his masculinity colored everything he did in intimate relationships, he held on to the hope that things would work out. However, he never thought of the possibility that he might have to rethink his images of what manhood meant and what marriage meant.

Multidirectional partiality helped each person to present his and her view of the presenting problem. I saw part of the problem as the need to become more realistic about their ideal image of marriage. I also saw the need for Mrs. P to develop her own life and not sacrifice it for the sake of Mr. P's need to keep his ideal image of himself. I saw his need to be more realistic about his self-image and revise his self-expectations and marital expectations. As I shared these observations, he still felt that the only thing he needed to do was to get his bonus and things would be all right. Mrs. P saw what she needed to do, and she decided to begin working on personal goals.

As the first three sessions with Mr. and Mrs. P progressed, it became apparent to me that there were some real good reasons for Mr. and Mrs. P responding the way they did toward each other. Some things that emerged in the assessment phase helped to put the problem into a larger perspective.

The crucial issue in joining with this couple had to do with engaging the real concerns of their marital relationship while at the same time not alienating the African American male. The compulsive masculinity concept, or believing that manhood revolves around being less relational and less feeling-oriented, is what keeps most African American men from counseling. Therefore, I had to make sure that I attended closely to his anxiety about having another male view his sexual impotency. Sometimes spouses get upset with the caution that I might employ in joining with the male. However, in this particular case, Mrs. P did not seem to be disturbed by my caution.

Assessment

In this section external, vertical, and horizontal factors will be explored in relation to the clarified problem.

External stressors concern bicultural, racial, economic, and religious issues. Religious issues move to the top of the list when dealing with the clarified problem of Mr. and Mrs. P. They had brought to their marriage very traditional ideas about the roles of men and women in marriage. If Mr. P had been able to live up to the role expectations for the male as sole provider, both would have been satisfied with their marital relationship. Religious values weighed heavily on their understanding of marriage and family life. The crisis related to Mr. P's inability to fulfill the traditional role, and this caused some cognitive dissonance or disorder in their image of the ideal marriage. Consequently, Mrs. P sought to move beyond the traditional ideal, while Mr. P sought to reinforce the ideal.

Racial discrimination and economic factors were also part of the complex picture, especially influencing Mr. P, who responded to this racial climate through the values of compulsive masculinity. He wanted the success held out by corporate America, but he also feared that he might be undermined in his quest by racial discrimination. Underlying this fear were feelings of low self-esteem and a negative view of self rooted in the fear that he could not meet the demands of the traditional male role.

Mrs. P, however, seemed less focused on success issues of the workplace. She seemed content with her job, but wanted to spend more effort developing her job skills.

Bicultural issues are related to economic factors with regard to Mr. P. He participated fully in wider cultural economic expectations without this participation being balanced by African American cultural concerns. His loyalty was to the marketplace. Therefore, his whole life was out of balance, and this exacerbated the compulsive masculine emphasis and fears of sexual and work impotency.

The vertical stressors related to the inheritances that each brought to the marriage from the family of origin also help to give focus to the clarified problem. Mrs. P came from a family of origin where her mother and father were divorced. She felt she was unwanted by her mother and received constant put-downs from her. She had a great deal of distrust for her mother and described her mother as abusive and nonnurturing. Mrs. P seemed familiar with putting her needs secondary and sacrificing her personal goals and happiness because of her family legacy. It seems that this pattern of sacrificing her needs and happiness for the sake of others was being repeated in her marriage.

Mr. P came from a background of poverty. He despised it. He said that one of his oldest sisters had to drop out of school in order to work to help the family barely make ends meet. He remembers, with bitterness, not having lunch money and nice clothes like his peers. He vowed to himself as a young child that he would never be poor. This desire to escape poverty became a burning motivation in his life, and he always made this a priority in his life. Everything else seemed to take a backseat to this concern.

Mr. P did all he could to be successful, but the values connected with compulsive masculinity surfaced. The values of compulsive masculinity are attaching very little value to work, sacrifice, self-improvement, or service to family, friends, or community.[4] While he had transcended these values most of the time, they were still part of his background. Sometimes they would surface in his life at crucial times and contribute to marital discord. At times living up to the expectations of being a traditional male appeared to be beyond his ability.

The clarified problem also needs to be understood in light of their developmental stages. They belonged to different life stages. Mr. P had very little empathy for the self-differentiation tasks that Mrs. P was wanting to address in her life. Mr. P would like her to continue to sacrifice herself for his sake and the sake of the family. He seemed to have very little awareness that Mrs. P was desiring to develop herself.

Mr. P was caught up in his own life cycle issues. He was in the beginning of his midlife crisis. He was constantly being forced to reevaluate his goals and aspirations by the marketplace. Yet he still held on to his desire for corporate success. Mrs. P seemed to resent his constant focus on success, and she felt she could live a far more modest life than he wanted. His tenacious holding on to his career ideals and self-expectations were delaying his coming to grips with his midlife realities.

Marital Assessment

Part of the assessment process involves evaluating the interaction taking place between Mr. and Mrs. P. The emotional climate between them was safe, but their relationship temperature was lukewarm; it was neither hot nor cold. Although they did not function as man and wife sexually, there did not appear to be any severe emotional conflict between them. Their companionship needs prevented them from severely undermining the other's self-esteem.

They possessed the ability to communicate frankly about their dissatisfactions. However, the major problem appeared to be the inability to be supportive of the other's individual growth needs. Mrs. P was engaged in the effort to become a separate self who was not dependent on her husband for everything. Mr. P found this threatening, and he openly expressed his disappointment to her. Mrs. P expressed that she felt her husband was chasing unrealistic pipe dreams and that he needed to become more realistic about his work and career. She would often say to him that he wanted to be number one in the corporate world or to chase unsuccessful business adventures to meet his own needs rather than the needs of the marriage or the family. Mr. P experienced this frankness as nonsupportive of him. Mrs. P had ceased providing emotional support for his business adventures, because she found he was throwing away money that the family could use for its needs. She said that she only wanted some consistency in paying the bills so that they did not have to live hand to mouth all the time. She also believed that she could best help herself if she disengaged from Mr. P's ambitions in order to work on her own personal development. She gave up any marital goals that she had, because she felt his business and career ambitions were his central passion.

There is a great deal of shared activity. They attend church together regularly and are very involved together in church activities. They see this as very important and find church attendance and participation fulfilling. They like their minister because she seems very interested in their marital problems and tries to help.

There is very little marital fusion, that is, they are not stuck together without each person having his or her own sense of self. Mr. P would prefer that Mrs. P be more fused with him and his goals, but she does not want any part of this. Early in their marriage she wanted to seek her self-identity through him and his career, but she recognized that this was not reciprocal.

Their present relationship can be described as disengaged rather than fused. They do not sleep in the same bedroom, and Mrs. P prefers a platonic style of marriage. This leaves her free to pursue her self-differentiation. She finds it comfortable being housemates without being sexual partners. Mr. P does not like this, but he accepts it because of his sexual impotency.

In parenting, there is reciprocal functioning. They both agree that the children's needs should not suffer because of their marital difficulty. Because they function as parents well, and they both share in this activity together well, Mrs. P sees no need for them to live separately. In their spousal relationship, there is no reciprocal functioning. He goes his way, and she goes her way.

There is very little toxic conflict around the major marital issues such as sex, parenting, and in-laws. They do not draw third parties into their marital difficulty in ways that intensify their marital problems. They talk their concerns over with their pastor or with me as their pastoral counselor. Occasionally, Mr. P makes negative remarks about women in Sunday school that hint at some marital problems. However, Mrs. P just shrugs this off as his childish personality. Although sex is a major problem, there is peaceful coexistence since Mr. P is impotent. Mrs. P does not seem to mind this, because this frees her to have more energy to invest in her own growth needs. Mr. P does not blame Mrs. P for his sexual problems, he does realize he has a problem. He is disappointed that his wife is not more upset with their sexual relationship. She did indicate in a private session that if there was a divorce between them, she would want to get remarried where sex would be important. However, her more immediate goal was to fulfill her career goals and put the marriage problems on hold.

In the area of marital paradigms, their marital mythology reflects a closed/traditional model of marriage. However, this traditional model is shifting for Mrs. P. She is moving more toward the random/individualistic model as a way not to sacrifice her own needs and career ambitions for the marriage. She would welcome participating in the traditional model if Mr. P had been different in his attitude and behavior, however. She had withdrawn her effort to support his self-esteem and is putting all her energy on self-differentiation.

Although Mr. and Mrs. P cannot work out their marital differences, their marital difficulties do not appear to have interfered with their functioning as parents. Their parental coalition seems very effective, and they do attend to their children's growth needs.

In the area of theological assessment of their marriage relationship and parenting skills, they seem to have two different types of models. Their spousal relationship is growth-inhibiting. Neither spouse supports the growth needs of the other. Mr. P refuses to affirm Mrs. P's needs for self-differentiation. Mrs. P has given up on supporting Mr. P's growth needs, because she found that this took too much from her own effort to be self-differentiated. Consequently, the holistic growth norm and the ethic of love are nonoperative in their marital relationship.

Their parenting relationship, however, does function according to the holistic growth norm and the ethic of love. They work together well, assuring that their children have the proper environment for their individual growth. Consequently, they appear to be staying together for the sake of their children and their children's needs.

It is not unusual to see parents in the closed/traditional model stay together for the sake of the children. This does reflect some of the religious values that exist in the communities from which they came. Moreover, it is not uncommon for African American families to have developed excellent parental coalitions while not having developed inadequate spousal reciprocity. This has been the observation of Salvador Minuchin in his book entitled *Families of the Slums.*[5] In many families he studied that had intact spousal subsystems, the spousal subsystem functioned as a parental subsystem.

The question from a pastoral theological point of view is, Should a marriage that functions as a parental subsystem rather than as a marital subsystem remain a marriage? My pastoral theological orientation informs me that this should be a major question that should be addressed with the couple. There is no propositional answer that can be given. Rather, the process answer needs to emerge from the couple with help from the pastoral counselor. I do feel that the question is central and cannot be ignored.

Mr. and Mrs. P struggled with this question in marital pastoral counseling. Their answer was that they felt that if the children's needs were being sacrificed because of their marital conflict, then they should separate and divorce. Theologically, the needs of the children were placed on a higher plain than their marital satisfaction.

In the area of sacrificing individual needs for the sake of the marriage, there was a different theological answer. Mrs. P was moving to the position that there should be a balance between meeting individual needs and marital needs. However, I think Mr. P felt that his personal needs should come first before the marital needs.

The norm of holistic growth and the ethic of love are important guides to informing the behavior of couples and families. How the norm and ethic inform what the therapist does in therapy needs to be examined. In the next section the major therapeutic interventions made with Mr. and Mrs. P surrounding this norm and ethic will be examined. The focus will be on how I as pastoral counselor helped them to reflect on their partiality toward parenting and their lack of balancing individual and marital needs.

The Stages of Marital Intervention

Goals of Marriage Therapy

I focused first on their spousal relationship in the goal-setting stage. I was influenced by my theological commitment to the norm of holistic liberated growth and the ethic of love. I was concerned that they be responsive to the growth needs of the other. While I did not explicitly state my theological values, I did use these values to help them to formulate their goals for marital therapy. Their goals included Mrs. P moving toward her self-differentiation goals, on the one hand, and decreasing Mr. P's anxiety about her increased autonomy. I indicated that I would support her move toward self-differentiation, because I felt that this would be in the best interest of their marital relationship in the long run. I also indicated to Mr. P that I would help him explore his career goals and their impact on the marriage. I also indicated that I was interested in how well they saw the world through the other's eyes. Therefore, mutual empathy was something that I hoped they would achieve. They indicated that they thought they would give the goals a try, although Mr. P expressed some disappointment that I was not going to reinforce the closed/traditional model of marriage. My feeling was that Mrs. P's self-differentiation goals were very important, and I thought it important that Mr. P explore whether or not he could tolerate her increased autonomy. I also thought that his becoming more empathic with his wife would help to alter his compulsive masculinity.

Another goal was to help them explore the closed/traditional model of marriage and help them to examine whether a different model responding to their realistic marital and family situation would be more appropriate. I also kept in my mind their lack of sexual intimacy, and I wanted to explore with them whether sacrificing their spousal relationship for parenting would be helpful to their marital relationship in the long run.

The Process of Pastoral Counseling

It would be helpful to examine some of the sessions of pastoral counseling to envisage how the established goals of therapy were addressed session by session. In the third and fourth sessions, following the goal-setting stage, the mistrust that Mr. and Mrs. P had toward each other surfaced. She distrusted his ability to fulfill his promises to make things better financially. She was a better manager of money than he, and they could make it all right financially if she managed the money. He admitted this, but he felt he would be giving up too much of himself if he let her handle the money. In the fifth and sixth sessions Mr. P's distrust of Mrs. P handling the money appeared to have sources prior to their marriage. He discovered that he had felt that if he did not control the money, they would end up as poor as his family of origin. In the fifth and sixth sessions, Mrs. P began to express that she was moving out of a personal depression. She said she no longer felt trapped in the relationship. She knew what she had to do to make her life happy, and she declared that she would pursue her personal goals. She said she was no longer going to wait for Mr. P to make her life happy. She would be taking her own happiness into her own hands.

In the seventh session Mr. P seemed to be going through some of the material related to the closed/traditional model. He would accuse her of not being there for him. Mrs. P indicated that she was tired of the hassles, and did not see herself falling back into the old patterns. She also began to make connections between the marital relationship and how her mother treated her. She saw herself moving to deal with family of origin issues as an important means of moving toward autonomy.

As Mrs. P began to move toward increased autonomy and self-differentiation, they both began to ask for individual sessions to work on personal issues. Mr. P began to accept his wife's disappointment in him, and he became less intimidated by her increased autonomy. In our separate sessions Mrs. P began to express that she really did not want a marital relationship with Mr. P. She did not want any sexual intimacy. She became clear that she wanted only a relationship for the sake of the children. She did indicate that if the children did become adversely affected by their marital problems, she would seek a divorce. When I explored with her why she did not seek a divorce since the spousal relationship was dead, she said it was convenient to stay married.

Mrs. P shared her concerns with Mr. P in a joint session. He was clearly disappointed. He said he wanted something more. However, he would settle for a parental focus of their marital relationship with hopes that this would change in the future.

Therapy ended around session twenty. They initiated the termination feeling that they had reached some peaceful coexistence. I expressed my concern that there were still issues related to family of origin concerns that made them comfortable with the platonic relationship. They acknowledged this but decided not to explore the family of origin issues any further.

My role was to help the couple to explore and clarify their marital relationship. A major area of reflection was their sacrifice of marital happiness in favor of their parenting role. I also helped them to explore family of origin issues that impacted their marital situation. I also explored with them the role of the closed/traditional model. In the end they chose a nontraditional model of staying together as long as it did not negatively influence the children. Mr. P reluctantly went along with this parenting focus hoping that Mrs. P would change her mind about the spousal relationship later on.

After a six-month period I had a follow-up visit with Mr. and Mrs. P. Nothing had changed about their marital and personal goals. There was still no sexual intimacy. However, they had increased their involvement with an African American congregation. This helped to bring a balance in the marketplace loyalty of Mr. P and his need for compulsive masculinity. The church was progressive with regard to the development of African American women, and this helped him to be more committed to Mrs. P's autonomy goals. He was becoming more relational, and there was a better balance between the egalitarian and androgynous roles and his marketplace orientation.

Conclusions

The aim of this chapter has been to illustrate the model of marriage and family therapy with African Americans in relationship to a particular case related to sexual dysfunction. As the case material unfolded, it became clear that the sexual problem was secondary, and the sacrifice of the spousal relationship for the parenting focus was the major problem. Using the norm of liberated holistic growth for each spouse, I explored with them how to be committed to their own growth and to the growth of the other. I also helped them to clarify the appropriateness of the parenting model as the focus of their marital relationship. I felt that they had to make the determination about the focus of their own marital relationship, but the theological norm and religious ethic influenced the kinds of questions I raised with them.

It was also pointed out that there is a tradition among African American couples to focus on parenting while neglecting their spousal relationship. The marital therapeutic bias is that the spousal relationship is primary to the parental coalition. Theologically, it is also important to explore how the spousal relationship impacts the parental coalition. This theological perspective helped me to explore with them the limitations of the final decision that they made about their parenting focus.

The theological perspective also helped me to focus with them on the closed/traditional model. It was obvious that this model was preventing both of them from achieving their individual needs as well as supporting the growth needs of the other spouse.

The model of joining, assessment, and intervention grounded in the theological norm of liberated holistic growth was very helpful in assessing and designing strategies for intervention with an African American couple.

Throughout my pastoral counseling with the couple the concern of compulsive masculinity was a major personal issue impacting everything that was done. The counseling dilemma had to do with how to help Mr. P join the marital counseling process and not scare him off. I tried to deal with this by providing a comfortable atmosphere of safety where he could realistically look at himself and the marriage. I had this concern at every session.

I did not think that I really made an impact on Mr. P's self-image. This would require longer personal therapy. He did not seem to want to move in the direction of personality change, and therefore, marital therapy remained the focus. My general conclusion is that many African American counselees stick to presenting problems and seldom move toward personal therapeutic goals. This observation is consistent with much of the literature on doing therapy with African Americans. This literature says that African Americans are problem-solving-oriented and task-oriented in the therapeutic process.

Chapter Eight

Marital Therapy and an Extramarital Affair

In this chapter, a case focusing on an extramarital affair will be presented to illustrate the use of the model. Two dimensions of the African American marital experience will be emphasized in this chapter. The first relates to the extramarital affair as a midlife crisis responding to the limitations of the closed/traditional model of marriage. The second is the role of compulsive masculinity in initiating an affair. The issues of compulsive masculinity surfaced as a way to compensate for significant losses that had been sustained in the African American male's life. Moreover, the concern of how internalized racism by a black wife and its role in extramarital relationships will be explored. A case will be presented focusing on a marriage where a wife's presenting problem was to deal with the extramarital affair of her husband.

The Case of Constance and Richard

I received a call from Constance saying that she had discovered her husband's car in front of the house of a female friend. When she asked her husband about the car and where he was, he admitted that he had had an affair. She was horrified and crushed. She had suspected his having affairs since the beginning of their marriage. However, this was the first time that she actually sought to find out the truth in an active way.

I asked her if her husband was interested in coming for marital therapy with her. She indicated that he was. I made an appointment to see her first, and then I made an appointment to see them both together.

This section will present an assessment and intervention for Constance and Richard as they struggled to decide what to do about their marital relationship. Constance was ambivalent about the marriage. *Ambivalent* refers to not being sure that she will stay or remain in the marriage.[1] On the one hand, she did not know whether she wanted to leave or stay at that point of the marital therapy. She was in the process of making up her mind. On the other hand, Richard was post-ambivalent-positive about the marriage. This means that he had made up his mind that he was in the marriage permanently and wanted it to work.[2] He said that he had given up the affair, and he would do whatever he had to do to hold on to the marriage. Consequently, they were in a holding pattern while Constance decided if she wanted to remain in the marriage. Richard was getting very uncomfortable waiting for her to make up her mind, however. This was because he felt that Constance's lashing out and bitterness toward the woman in the affair was out of place and dangerous.

Brief Marital History

Richard met Constance when they were in college. He got her pregnant, and they decided to get married.

At the time of the therapy, he worked in the corporate world in upper management. She worked in the health-related field in a supervisory capacity.

They have had sex only a few times in the last two years. She felt that this was his preference.

His health was fine, but she had problems with her stomach. This required surgery that interrupted the pastoral counseling.

He said that the current affair in question was with a distant acquaintance and that the affair ended almost as fast as it began. He said that he knew that this was not what he wanted when he engaged in the affair. Initially Constance distrusted his truthfulness. She was very hurt because the woman was younger than she.

The Joining Effort

Constance contacted me by phone and was very desperate. I ascertained from her the concerns she had. She told me of the affair and how desperate and angry she was. I made an appointment to see her the next day.

I saw Constance alone for the first session. I spent most of the time attending to her feelings about the affair and building a relationship with her. I took as much history surrounding the presenting problem as I could. She indicated that Richard wanted to come to the therapy sessions.

In the second session I saw them together. I spent most of the time getting a history from Richard. I felt I had to be very careful and move very slowly with him. I had to work very hard to build a relationship with him and not convey to him any feelings of judgment or condemnation. My agenda in this session was to create an atmosphere where he felt he could give his side of the story without having to be prejudged. He was very co-operative and articulate. I did feel that I was doing multidirectional partiality, and I did this to make sure I attended to his point of view.

He volunteered that he was guilty of the offense and was willing to suffer whatever consequences there were as a result. He said he knew the affair was wrong as soon as it occurred, and he indicated that it was over as fast as it started. He commented that he saw what he really wanted in life, and he did not want to live his life in a lie.

In the third session we explored Constance's anger that was buried and denied for many years prior to the affair. Up until a week before this session, the anger was not apparent at all. Most of the time she expressed her anger by withdrawing into her work. However, she exploded between the second and the third session. She ripped out his private phone; she called the woman with whom Richard had had the affair. The anger and hurt were very deep.

He expressed alarm at her behavior, and he felt that this was no way to repair a broken relationship. He indicated that her behavior felt very uncomfortable to him. Her response was that the woman expressed to her that she should confine her talking with Richard and not draw her into the middle of their problem. Richard agreed with the woman's attitude. Constance got delight out of seeing Richard so uncomfortable. I explored with her how her direct contact with the woman in the affair might present added problems for her relationship with her husband. I explored with Constance whether her effort was counterproductive, especially since her husband said he had given up the relationship with the woman. He gave assurances that the affair was over. She did not seem convinced that the relationship was over. At the end of the third session she had not stopped contacting the woman.

Later in that session I summarized how I saw their relationship and their interaction. I shared with them what I could do to help them improve their relationship. She expressed ambivalence about the future of their relationship, and Richard said that he was committed to making their relationship work. They both agreed to continue to come to therapy, however.

In summary, the joining effort took three sessions, during which I was able to join them through multidirectional partiality. Through this skill, the presenting problem was reviewed and clarified. This laid the grounds for the middle phase of pastoral counseling where Constance would make up her mind whether she wanted to stay married and whether Richard could continue to be present while she made up her mind. The middle phase of pastoral counseling will be explored later beginning with the fourth session with Richard and Constance.

In the joining process, I did not have to be as cautious about Richard's male ego. He seemed very capable of facing squarely any flaws that he had in his personality. It seemed as if the crisis enabled him to evaluate his fragile male ego, and he decided that he had to become more responsible in his behavior and to be more emotionally mature. However, Constance's ego was temporarily shattered by the affair, and I needed to be cautious with her to make sure her ego was secure.

In my joining effort, I stayed with the presenting problem. From experience I recognize that many of my African American couples stay fairly close to the presenting problem, and many rarely venture into exploring depth psychological reasons for their problems. Efforts to move into the direction of their personal and depth psychological concerns can only come after periods of attending to the marital problems and the couple realizes that there is need to do some individual work. This rarely happens, however, because many terminate once they feel that the marital problem is resolved to their satisfaction.

From the beginning Richard felt that he was aware of his motivation for what he did and that he could in time correct things. It was clear to me that neither of them was concerned to go into any deeper reasons or family of origin issues regarding their marital conflict. They resisted efforts to move into individual issues in depth. This is very common with most of the couples with whom I do marital counseling. This is consistent with the findings in the literature of doing pastoral counseling with African American couples.

External Assessment

An important part of the cultural assessment is the marital mythology that each person brings to the marriage. It is important to look at the marital mythology influencing their relationship. Marital mythology relates to the ideal mate image and expectation that each spouse brings to the marital dyad.[3] Constance brought to the mating and formation stage of the relationship an expectation of an ideal mate who would protect, comfort, and make decisions for her as her father did. Richard brought to the mating and formation stage an expectation of a mate who would not challenge his authority and who would give him personal space. They seemed to form a contract based on these expectations of the other which went unchallenged until the affair.

Closely related to the ideal mate image of Constance and Richard were the explicit African American cultural images of male and female relationships. One major image of male and female relationships in this culture is the expectation that the male provides for the female and children while he maintains his aloofness from the family. A related major image is that the female is expected to give her life completely over to the male and to forget her self-focus. This latter social expectation accounted for Constance's adoption of the adaptive-passive position. The former cultural expectation also accounts for Richard's negative reaction to any change in the relationship. In other words, they had a closed/traditional marriage where they played traditional and stereotypical male and female roles.

A bicultural concern for Richard was the world of compulsive masculinity and the relational world of his mother. He often stated that the caring and relational world of his mother helped him to keep perspective on what was real and unreal for his life. The more he got involved with compulsive masculinity the more alienated he was from his mother's values and African American culture.

A bicultural concern for Constance had to do with internalized racism related to skin color and size. While she only hinted at these issues, their stay in therapy did not permit me to explore these concerns in depth. Constance did not meet the standards of European beauty held out by wider society. She did have light skin, but her age and size did not fit the stereotypical images of white women's beauty. It is acknowledged that the standard of beauty in the African American community is different from that of wider society. However, self-hatred in terms of body image did play a role in how Constance felt about the affair. For example, Cheryl Townsend Gilkes points out:

> In spite of the high premium placed on culturally exalted images of white female beauty and the comedic exploitation that surrounds the large Black women, many African-Americans know that the most respected image of Black women, within and outside of the community, is that of the large women. Although it is respected, it is a culturally deviant image that is not necessarily loved. It is an image of power in a community where women need to be fortified and empowered.[4]

Gilkes continues:

> It is an asexual image that sometimes permits escape from the constant harassment and sexual aggression, accurately called "hitting on," that disproportionately pervade the lives of those Black women who most approximate white cultural ideals. In the era of "fitness and health," that same image is officially labeled "obese" and makes every large Black woman an immediately suspected case of bulimia.[5]

The affair of Richard with a younger woman made Constance preoccupied with her body image although she did not say very much about her feelings in this area. She felt secure that she was the marrying kind because she knew her husband preferred large women. However, his lack of attention to her physically caused her to feel that she was not necessarily the one with whom her husband wanted sex. The concern of asexuality raised in the excerpt also was below the surface in her mind, and therapy did not last long enough to get at this issue. When they felt comfortable enough that the crisis was over, they terminated therapy.

Vertical Assessment

Three-Generation Genogram

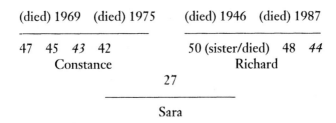

(died) 1969   (died) 1975   (died) 1946   (died) 1987

47   45   *43*   42   50 (sister/died)   48   *44*
       Constance   Richard

                        27

                      Sara

There are several key things about the genogram that have bearing on their marital relationship. Richard had a very close relationship with the sister who was six years older than he. He was closer to her than anyone else. She had cancer and suffered for five years. He grieved a lot for her and still grieves some today. He began the affair in the last year of her life.

Constance was very close to her father. He never approved of her marriage to Richard and was very devastated by the marriage to him. She also married close to the time her mother died.

Certain marital patterns were rooted in the nondifferentiated continuance of each spouse's family of origin patterns. Constance seemed to want to continue the father-daughter relationship she had with her deceased father, and Richard seemed to be content to remain distant from a controlling and disciplinary mother figure. He seemed to be able to manipulate his mother by charming her and never really letting her see the negative side of himself. He survived his mother by hiding his real self and allowing his mother to think of him as an angel. Consequently, he sought to marry someone who would not place any emotional demands on him and a person whom he could charm. He wanted someone who would give him space as well. Both seemed to have fit each other's ideal mate expectations. They formed their contract based on these mutual expectations, and they lived this contract out comfortably until the affair was discovered. The affair caused a disruption in their long-term contract or agreement.

Richard seemed to have good contact with others, including his friends, extended family, and in-laws. However, he tended to be an overfunctioner in that he seemed to carry a lot of the relationships by his own efforts. People looked to him for leadership and advice. He seemed to invest a lot of time playing the father role for Constance's brother and sisters. However, his close contact with his own extended family had slipped since his sister's death. He did not want to be reminded of her death when he visited his other brothers and sisters.

Constance seemed not to have many important relationships. She had friends at work, but these relationships did not go beyond occasional lunches. She did not seem to have special friends. Consequently, she was very vulnerable when their daughter left the home and her husband had the affair.

Horizontal Stressor:
Marital Stage

Constance and Richard's marital relationship had progressed through the mating and formation phase where they worked on the initial tasks of developing commitment, caring communication, conflict/compromise, and developing a working contract.[6] They had also passed through the expansion phase where they had a daughter and had launched her. They had also gone through the stage of contraction where Sara, their daughter, had individuated and become her own person. They seemed to be in their postparental stage where the tasks included supporting each other's attempts to find meaning, satisfaction, and productivity, maintaining a satisfactory degree of closeness, deepening communication, developing capacity to deal with loss of productivity, and supporting each other in the face of possible losses.

It was clear to me that both Constance and Richard were facing midlife crises. Constance was moving very well in her career and felt that she did not have to continue to live in a closed/traditional paradigm.[7] Their closed/traditional paradigm was a pattern where Richard and Constance performed stereotypical gender roles with Richard as clearly dominant. Constance felt the need to move out of the domination of her husband. She no longer looked to him for answers to her problems as she once did.

Richard was also facing a midlife crisis. He was exploring things he wanted to do with the remainder of his life. At forty-four he no longer wanted to continue in the same job and lifestyle in the future. It appeared that the extramarital affair was his attempt to experiment with a dangerous, but alternative style of life that was different from the closed/traditional paradigm. He too seemed tired of the closed/traditional paradigm. This was a clear indication that a second order of change (change in dominant marital pattern) was something they might want.

The midlife crisis of males is rooted in a search for deeper spiritual roots.[8] From the perspective of male and female roles, there is often a shift or a reversal of roles away from the closed/traditional paradigm; that is, the husband moves inward to find strength for the future, and the female moves outward to the work world and career. It seemed that Constance was right on time based on the midlife transition data while Richard seemed to be resisting the transition. The affair was his feeble attempt to resolve or avoid dealing with the tasks of midlife. Perhaps his resolve to make decisions about his future in the marriage and job in the near future represents a more mature attempt to deal with this transition period.

Of significance was the fact that Richard temporarily returned to aspects of compulsive masculinity initially to help him deal with midlife transitions. That is to say, he moved into sexual exploits and conquests, which are characteristic of one aspect of compulsive masculinity. However, as soon as he did it, he realized that he had outgrown this phase of his life. He was clear that he did not want to return to this lifestyle.

Constance seemed to want to change the marital relationship. When she was less ambivalent, she wanted more from the marriage and could not tolerate the marriage continuing to exist in the same old pattern. Richard seemed to be going along with Constance's wants and expectations, but it was not clear whether he was ready for a different style of marital relationship beyond the closed/traditional model.

So far the assessment has not emphasized many African American concerns. However, how Richard responded to the midlife crisis and the loss of a significant family member set the stage for his responding to the midlife crisis through compulsive masculinity. Compulsive masculinity was a factor in Richard's decision to have an affair. As a response to racism compulsive masculinity is an attempt to deal with any blow to the self-esteem through appearing tough, detached, and by sexual exploits. While racism was not a major factor in the affair for Richard, there was a blow to his self-image due to the aging process and the sudden loss of a family member to whom he was very close. Consequently, the affair was a response to circumstances related to aging and loss.

The Marital Dyad

The marital stage analysis revealed that their marriage was in the postparental phase. It will be helpful to explore issues concerning the marital dyad, including the emotional climate, communication, relationship time and activity together, personal boundaries, personal styles of interaction (pursuer-distancer), and power and influence in their relationship.[9]

The emotional climate relationship atmosphere between Constance and Richard was threatening and unsafe; the temperature was hot and cold; and there was the presence of an active turbulent conflict. Early in counseling Constance was still in the process of discovering and expressing her anger, hurt, rage, and bitterness at being betrayed by Richard. Richard was also very angry but in a very controlled way. He was angry that Constance had reacted with intense hostility to the affair. He was upset because her actions were unpredictable and she seemed bent on destroying him. He was more comfortable when her behavior became less hostile and more consistent. He was so used to her not expressing her anger and keeping her opinions to herself.

The communication or exchange of information between them drastically shifted after the affair. Prior to the affair, there was rarely open expression of feelings between them. She never raised any dissatisfaction that she had with him or her suspicions about his affairs. She suffered quietly, withdrew, and would not communicate.

Richard favored very little self-disclosure. He rarely shared his inner feelings with Constance. He said he kept things to himself and worked them out within himself. He preferred that strong feelings not be shared at all between them. This was reinforced by his nonverbal posture and facial expressions disapproving the expression of strong feelings.

It seemed that their communication was not critical, laudatory, or affectionate. Even in therapy, they made considerable effort not to be critical of each other. They avoided confrontation. It was very difficult to get them to share their feelings. They overcontrolled both negative and positive feelings. They seemed to act their feelings out more than talk about them.

Since discovering the affair, Constance had become much more aggressive in her pursuit of questions about the affair. Richard's reaction was to withhold information and withdraw. He did not want to share anything about the affair. He only shared that it was over and warned Constance not to try to find out anything about it. This withholding fed Constance's suspicion and forced her to become more aggressive to find out what she wanted to know. She also intercepted his mail, read his mobile phone bills, and looked for anything that could put pieces of the affair together. She was trying to confirm her suspicion that the affair was not over.

Constance distrusted everything that Richard said. He had no credibility at all with her. Credibility refers to the amount of trust that each partner has in the other. Richard also distrusted Constance because of her hostile and aggressive behavior. He viewed her as angry, vengeful, and wanting to embarrass him. He believed that she would even embarrass herself in order to punish him. Because of her unpredictability, Constance's credibility with him was very low.

They had had very little time and activity together since the wedding. He was very involved in his work. Even on the weekends, he was busy doing things outside the home rather than putting time into the relationship. She seemed happy with this up until she discovered the infidelity.

The discussion will now turn to personal boundaries. Personal boundaries refer to levels of differentiation that each spouse has and the amount of emotional space each needs to maintain a degree of personal comfortableness. It seemed that both Richard and Constance required a great deal of emotional distance from each other. Both needed the current pattern of distance to maintain a sense of personal well-being. Personal well-being refers to the amount of attention and creativity given to one's own emotional and physical well-being.

A dominant and submissive pattern of interaction existed between them. She seemed to have needed someone who could give direction to her life and make the major decisions for her. He seemed to be comfortable with this pattern.

A pursuer and distancer pattern was at work as well. Prior to the affair or during the premorbid state of the marriage (prior to the current conflict), the pursuer and distancer pattern between them was dormant. They were happy keeping a certain fixed distance between them. The discovery of the affair, however, set in motion a deadly pursuit and distance phase in their relationship. When Constance discovered the affair, she became the pursuer of details of the affair as well as looking for evidence that the affair was continuing. She demanded to know about the affair and wanted more self-disclosure from Richard. As she pursued, he distanced himself. As he distanced, the more intense her pursuit became. Finally, she got frustrated and tired, but she did not give up the pursuit immediately. He tried to respond positively to her pursuit, but she rebelled.

The affair had not only brought on the pursuer and distancer pattern, it also disrupted the dominant and submissive pattern. It disturbed the power arrangement between them. Constance made more of a claim for making decisions for her own life. She demanded fidelity from Richard. Richard had never been accountable to Constance for anything that he had done in the past, and she began holding him accountable. Richard was not sure he wanted this kind of relationship although he said he did.

Triangles

The depth of the marital dysfunction between Richard and Constance can be discerned by giving attention to the triangles in their relationship.[10] Anxiety results in the pained marital relationship that cannot be contained by it. Consequently, a third party is drawn into the pained marital relationship in order to stabilize the dyad. This process of drawing a third party into the relationship to lessen the anxiety is called a triangulation.

Triangles function to externalize the marital dyad conflict. This means that the anxiety internal to the marital dyad gets pushed outside itself. The affair that Richard had was the most obvious triangle impacting their marital dyad. The triangle involved drawing someone outside the family into the middle of their marital relationship. This affair functioned to maintain the steady state of the marital dyad up until the time that the affair was discovered.

In addition to the "obvious affair triangle" there was a "counteraffair triangle." For years Constance has participated in an internal family triangle with her daughter. She had gotten overly involved with the mothering task. Even when the affair was exposed, their twenty-six-year-old daughter wanted to come take care of her.

Richard's work was another external triangle in which he participated. In addition to the affair and work, there was a triangle between the sister who died and Richard. This was an extended-family triangle where Richard seemed to tolerate the closeness with another person that he could not tolerate in the marriage. There was a connection between grieving for his sister and the affair in Richard's case.

The fact that there were several interconnecting triangles at work in their relationship meant that the triangles were interlocking. All of them interlocked and seemed to fulfill the same function, which was to lessen the pressure on the marriage.

The Spouses
as Individuals

Mention has already been made of the level of differentiation existing in the lives of Richard and Constance. Both seemed to have brought significant family of origin issues into their marital relationship. These patterns seemed to be repeated in the marital dyad. It seemed that they both formed a collusion between them that each would maintain the other's family of origin pattern. In this sense they were not well differentiated as individuals.

Another level of analysis of each spouse's personal functioning is represented by the Personal Functioning Index.[11] This index includes categories of productivity, relationships, and personal well-being.

Productivity relates to functioning well in one's job. Both Richard and Constance seemed to be very productive. Constance has received a promotion. Although Richard was unhappy with his job, the unhappiness was due to a change in leadership.

Neither seemed to know how to invest time and energy in their own personal well-being. They did not seem to look to caring for their own emotional needs in helpful and creative ways. Constance also seemed to lack interest in caring for her own physical needs. She had chronic leg pain, but she seemed resigned to it rather than seeking to resolve the problem through surgery. Richard seemed to care about his physical well-being more than Constance cared for her own. Eventually, she was forced into surgery, because of the severity of the injured leg.

The individual lives of marital partners also include the relationship position that each has in relationship to the other. Richard's relational position was the reactive position. His response to tension in the relationship was to distance himself while thinking that Constance was trying to take over and control his life.

Constance took more the adaptive position. In the past, she knuckled under to his program and was satisfied doing this until the affair. Prior to the affair, Richard seemed to be the overfunctioner in the relationship and Constance was the underfunctioner who let Richard run her life. This reciprocal pattern changed due to the affair, and this made Richard react.

Neither seemed to be in the self-focused position. Neither was taking the "I position." Constance projected blame. On the one hand, Richard seemed to accept his responsibility for the affair, but, on the other hand, he had not developed any real personal goals related to his midlife crisis. Richard had indicated that he was in the process of making some self-focused decisions. Perhaps he was increasing his responsibility for resolving the midlife crisis. Constance reluctantly moved toward self-focus, but she needed to do less projecting of blame.

In summary, the conflict between Constance and Richard is severe; however, there was no engagement of a lawyer for divorce proceedings because Constance is still ambivalent.

The relationship can be summarized as follows: (1) There is the presence of cluster stress—the marriage is in the postparental phase while both Richard and Constance are in the midst of midlife crises. *Cluster stress* relates to being in several different transitions and crises at the same time. (2) There is a lot of hostility and turbulence, and the environment is unsafe. (3) The exchange of information increased, but the pattern of withdrawing and distancing suddenly changed to open conflict and the expression of bitterness. There was increased emotional reactivity by them both. (4) Credibility had gone and the criticism each has of the other is slowly emerging. (5) There was some increase in activity together, but the dominant and submissive pattern had been challenged. (6) Self-focus was increasing for Richard, but Constance still projected blame rather than looking to what she wanted to do with her future life. (7) They both moved toward post-ambivalent-positive feelings. (8) And, finally, there were active triangles that could not be contained within the marital dyad.

From the African American perspective compulsive masculinity surfaced as one of the causes of the extramarital affair, that is, Richard responded to his midlife crisis issues by regressing to the sexual conquest phase of compulsive masculinity. He discovered quickly that Constance was not going to tolerate this behavior nor did he find this behavior fruitful. While she may have had feelings about being passed over for a younger woman, she would not accept being married to a husband who was having an affair. She was not going to play the female who held on to her man at any cost.

An additional African American issue relates to whether or not Richard and Constance would go beyond the behavioral marital problem and attend to some of the individual family of origin problems that were implicated in the problem. It was clear that Richard and Constance were interested mostly in getting the presenting problem of the affair attended to without moving toward some of the unconscious motivation for the problem.

The Middle Phase of Pastoral Counseling and Termination

Earlier in this chapter the joining phase of pastoral counseling was explored. The first three sessions were examined as a result. This section begins with the fourth session.

In the fourth session I began to explore with Constance the new promotion that she received at work. The conversation soon shifted to her relationship with Richard. Constance seemed to be less ambivalent about the marital relationship. She seemed to want to make some improvement in their relationship. Consequently, I moved with what I thought was her renewed commitment to the relationship. However, I received a call from her during the week, and she indicated I had assumed the wrong thing. She said she was still not sure what she wanted to do.

In the fifth session I had her explain her ambivalent feelings to her husband based on her phone call to me. He responded that he was in the process of reevaluating his own response to the continued commitment to their relationship. It appeared that he was moving from the post-ambivalent-positive position to a post-ambivalent-negative position. He seemed frustrated that she continued with her distrust of him and of his untrustworthy words. In later sessions she seemed to feel that Richard was genuine in his efforts to fulfill the promises that he made. Consequently, she became post-ambivalent-positive, and they initiated termination in the pastoral counseling.

In summary, the therapy sessions have served to (1) clarify the presenting problem, (2) take their marital and extended family relationship history, (3) get a glimpse of each spouse's personality resources and dynamics, and (4) clarify the nature of the ambivalence that each spouse brought to therapy.

My role as a pastoral counselor involved the following: (1) clarifying the presenting problem, (2) attending to the ambivalence about the marital commitment, (3) exploring the dominant and submissive patterns and the distancer and pursuer patterns, (4) trying to move toward self-focus for each spouse, (5) exploring family of origin relationships, and (6) some examination of the affair and counteraffair issue.

The sessions progressed to the point where Richard reached self-focus about his responsibility for his activity in the affair. Constance had given up the projection of blame and became more self-focused.

My immediate goals in pastoral counseling were to help Richard continue self-focusing as well as to increase his tolerance for Constance's anger; to help Constance to explore the history of bitterness related to disappointment in fulfillment of expectations; to help her move toward self-focus about what she wanted for her life so she could move toward the marriage or divorce.

Another subgoal was to establish a workable trust rather than a naive trust between them. This meant that both needed to clarify their expectations of the other as well as work on skills of commitment, caring, communication, and conflict/compromise.

Another goal was to help Richard to revisit the values and culture of his mother. His mother's outlook on the world seemed to be a good balance between the traditional relational values of the African American community and compulsive masculinity. Therefore, the more he could return home to build relationships with other members of his family, the more his mother's influence would impact him. He thought that this returning home might be beneficial to him at some point.

Theological Assessment

The major theological issue that needs to be addressed is the analysis of extramarital affairs in light of the norm of liberated holistic growth and the ethic of love. This calls for the assessment to go beyond propositional theology that prohibits adultery and move to an examination of the impact of adultery on the growth and development of both partners in the marriage. Propositional laws against adultery may seem to be arbitrary and put a damper on human freedom and expression. Yet when the impact of it on actual lives is understood, values prohibiting adultery make sense.

The norm of liberated holistic growth focuses on individuals maximizing their own emotional, psychological, interpersonal, and spiritual growth while also facilitating similar growth in others. The love ethic gives further emphasis on facilitating "other growth." In the case of the extramarital affair where Richard was the violator and Constance was the victim, their individual growth and their growth as a couple were severely challenged.

Both Richard and Constance were regular churchgoers and participants in the life of the church. Richard said that he had a very bad conscience, and recalled having images come to his awareness of his dead mother's disappointment at his behavior. Constance felt that Richard committed an unforgivable sin against her, and she did not know whether she could overcome this. She felt she had the weight of religious tradition on her side for her to condemn Richard's behavior.

The norm of liberated growth and the love ethic permeated the entire pastoral counseling process and gave shape to the interventions that I made. They gave guidance to the exploration of how the extramarital affair undermined spouses' personality growth, and how it undermined the marital subsystem through triangulation.

With regard to how the norm and ethic influenced my responses, I recognized that Constance's rage at Richard was justified. I recognized that he needed to hear the depth of her hurt while he sat present through it. I knew his presence was needed while she expressed the hurt and pain. His presence was essential for her reparation of the damage that the event did to undermine her personhood. I therefore encouraged her to express all of her pain, and I encouraged Richard to listen to it. I knew this would lay the foundation for repairing Constance's self-esteem.

I also realized that Richard had guilt that he needed to deal with for his own growth and development. I was sensitive to how Constance might have felt listening to his guilt around violated marital vows. I ascertained from her whether I should talk with Richard alone about his guilt. She said that she wanted to be present during whatever he had to say. She believed that this would help her to make up her mind about what she would eventually do about staying in the marriage.

The point is that I made their growth as individuals primary. This was the influence of the norm and ethic. I also was concerned for their marital relationship. Therefore, I explored with Richard the drawing of a third party into their marital situation. My concern for the marital relationship is also influenced by the norm and the ethic. Richard responded by saying that he was not unhappy with the marital relationship. He felt that the extramarital affair had nothing to do with his happiness or unhappiness with the marriage. Rather, he felt it related more to his personal life. However, he refused to make any excuses for his behavior. He realized that his behavior was wrong, and he did not want to insult Constance by offering any excuses.

Richard explored the impact of the extramarital affair on his personal growth. Up until the affair, he did not realize that he was not dealing realistically with his midlife crisis. Having the affair helped him to suddenly realize that his life needed to be assessed and that he needed to make some major adjustments in it. He admitted his shortcomings, and he discussed with his wife what he needed to do about getting his personal life together. Therefore, the norm and ethic that permeated the pastoral counseling relationship helped Richard to transform the negative affair into something positive for growth.

It was this latter commitment of Richard to his personal growth that was the foundation for the increase of Richard's credibility with Constance. Over the months she saw that he was serious about dealing with his personal concerns and getting his life on the right track. She found that her anger and bitterness began to lessen and her lack of commitment to herself began to change as well. They decided to terminate the sessions. I felt that their initiation of termination was premature; yet they seemed determined to work on personal growth things. The changes they were making in their individual lives could very easily lead to changes in the marriage.

In summary, the norm of liberated growth and the love ethic were implicit and explicit influences throughout the pastoral counseling with Richard and Constance. Moreover, the model used for joining, assessment, and intervention seemed adequate for addressing the concerns of extramarital affairs. It lent itself to process issues related to extramarital concerns while propositional concerns were not minimized.

Chapter Nine

Abuse and Pastoral Counseling

Balancing self-love and other love is the theological issue most prominent in cases of sexual abuse, physical abuse, and violence in marriages and families. Abuse represents the failure of self and other love. *Abuse* is the attempt to gain a sense of meaning and value at the expense of the growth and well-being of another. Abuse is the willingness to sacrifice the growth of another in order to secure one's own growth. Victimization by abuse often leads to self-abuse where one learns self-hatred and to sacrifice one's self-growth. This kind of abuse can be perpetrated by either men or women. However, in a patriarchal-oriented society, male abuse of females is more prevalent.

Abuse by African American men toward African American women must be understood from the perspective of compulsive masculinity. Here violence is understood as a way to defend the self from devaluation. The compulsive nature of masculinity surfaces and makes it difficult for some African American males to live in intimate relationships with females. Many African American men are very sensitive about their male image among females, and some are prone to use violence toward females if they feel degraded by them in any way. Sometimes emotional withdrawal and sexual withholding by their female partners are interpreted as degrading and a cause for violence.

While African American men respond with violence to being devalued, it is important to examine briefly how African American women respond to being devalued. Often African American women and men have internalized the devaluation of African American women by certain gender values held in wider society. Certain wider society gender norms figure greatly in the abuse and exploitation of African American women. Gilkes has identified these norms:

These norms include narrow European standards of beauty, a model of marriage and motherhood that enforces economic dependence, and social and intellectual subordination. Violation of these norms brings about the exclusion and punishment of women in a variety of ways. African American women, by choice and by circumstance, violate nearly every dimension of American gender norms. Failure to meet society's beauty norms is, in Schur's terms, "visual deviance." Visual conformity in the United States, of course, is tied to an idolatry of whiteness. For this opposition, they are assaulted from outside their communities, but African American women who are too dark face an outrageous complex of attitudes and behaviors from within their own communities.[1]

Both African American men and women are influenced by the cultural humiliation of African American women by the internalization of the gender norms. Such internalization is the source of physical, psychological, and emotional assaults against African American women by African American men. Moreover, African American women internalize these norms to self-degradation and self-destruction. More precisely, the African American community has blamed African American women for being the source of contemporary problems, according to Gilkes, and African American women have internalized this blame.[2] Because of this internalization, African American women have ignored their own needs for self-development and care for self to wage a war on behalf of African American men. The point is that many African American women are very vulnerable to abuse and exploitation because of the internalization of gender norms of wider society.

African American males have internalized the same gender norms and have difficulty with accepting the beauty of black women. Cornel West says:

> I do believe that deep down in the depths of the Black male psyche is a struggle with taking seriously the beauty of Black women. The ideals of White beauty, when it comes to women, are so deeply inscribed in every male psyche, Black and white, that many brothers do have problems acknowledging Black beauty, and by beauty I don't mean simply physical beauty.[3]

The primary focus of this chapter will be on a couple where physical abuse became a growing concern. In this case the potential of violence from the husband against the wife was very real. Moreover, the case raises some real concerns about whether African American marital partners need to be seen individually in order to give structure to the marital difficulty and to keep conflict between spouses manageable. Here one of the more subtle differences between many African American couples and other middle-class non-African American couples emerges. That is to say, this particular couple and many other African American couples whom I have had in couple pastoral counseling prefer to be seen together rather than separately.

Also some theological concerns are raised by African American womanist theologians about abuse. Attending to these theological concerns initially is important.

Theological Concerns

Some theologians have traced notions of abuse to the willingness to sacrifice others for the sake of self, and find this in the gospel itself. Womanist theologian Delores Williams has made such a theological conclusion. Drawing on African American women's experiences with racism, she uses the metaphor of surrogacy to lift up how abuse is related to the gospel:

> In this sense Jesus represents the ultimate surrogate; he stands in the place of someone else; sinful humankind. Surrogacy attached to divine personage, thus takes on an aura of the sacred. It is, therefore, fitting and proper for black women to ask whether the image of a surrogate-God has salvific power for black women or whether this image supports and reinforces the exploitation that has accompanied their experience with surrogacy. If black women accept this idea of redemption, can they not also passively accept the exploitation that surrogacy brings?[4]

Williams moves on to raise significant questions about whether Jesus on the cross represents coerced surrogacy that focuses on the willingness of God the Father to sacrifice the Son. She also wonders if this sacrifice was voluntary surrogacy where Jesus chose to be a surrogate himself. She further questions whether African Americans can gain salvation from the notion of the self-giving love when the experience of African American women with surrogacy is forced substitution for others. She also challenges the notions of atonement formulated by such names as ransom, satisfaction, and substitution.[5] Her conclusion is that salvation does not depend on any form of surrogacy made sacred by the orthodox Christian understanding of Jesus' life or death. She feels that salvation is assured by Jesus' resistance and his own survival struggle used to prevent the death of his identity.[6] She goes on to say that redemption must be freed from the cross and its related patriarchal ideas that have shaped classical theories of atonement. In essence, she holds that classical atonement theories reinforced the image of a patriarchal God who sacrificed his own Son for the sake of others. In Williams's mind, this reification lends itself to the abuse of women. Her basic conclusion is as follows:

> What this allows the womanist theologian to show black women is that God did not intend the surrogacy roles they have been forced to perform. God did not intend the defilement of their bodies as white men put

them in the place of white women to provide sexual pleasure for white men during the slavocracy. This is rape. Rape is defilement and defilement, and defilement means wanton desecration.[7]

My agreement with Delores Williams is at the level of the misuse of atonement theories to support the suppression of women. The value of her conclusions is related to her ability to show that the various theories of atonement were drawn from the metaphors prevalent at the time that these theories were constructed. She feels that these metaphors served a use for their context, but are inadequate for today. Therefore, she looks for better metaphors that grow out of the contemporary experiences of African Americans today.

Jacquelyn Grant also says that from a black Christian woman's perspective Jesus liberated black women while black women were liberating Jesus from racist, sexist, and classist encapsulation. She believes in a mutual liberation theory of atonement where the cross is freed from ideas related to abuse.[8]

The role of Jesus is so essential to the lives of African American women, and Williams has developed her theory of atonement in a way that would keep the centrality of Jesus and free African American women from surrogacy roles. She has done this by deemphasizing the cross as the center of atonement theories, and placing emphasis on righting relationships and the power of the resurrection to release God's Spirit and power in the world. For her, the cross did not produce salvation, but it was a sign of the presence of evil in the world that was overcome through the resurrection.[9] Williams's views on atonement are not an attack on Christology as some conservative theologians have thought. Rather, her views are an attempt to free Christology from a theory of surrogacy that enslaves women.

I recognize the limitations of the theology of the cross as understood from the surrogacy of African American women. However, the cross is important in my own theology. When I reflect on what I have written in the past about the cross, I discover that I have not used the surrogacy views of atonement. Rather, I reflect on 1 Corinthians 1:18–31 and put this passage on the foolishness of the cross into a narrative framework.[10] My theology of the cross relates more to the cross as cultural foolishness and a reversal of exploitative and oppressive value systems that placed power, exploitation, and worldly wisdom over against the wisdom of God. Therefore, I conclude that the cross is important from a reversal view of atonement in the new age.

Paul did not have the modern understanding in mind when he wrote about wisdom and the new age to come. Rather, he seemed to have in mind the new era that Jesus Christ had inaugurated. In this new age, things were reversed. In the new age the first became last and the last became first. The compassionate and humble became models for Christian leadership; the ruthless and powerful were models of sin and failure. The foolish by ordinary standards became wise, and the ones who lived by the world's standards became foolish. To pursue a Christian life was to subscribe to a new and different measure of success. Paul wanted the early Christians to realize that the power of the new age was transforming for those who were united in Christ.[11]

Understanding the reversal theory of atonement places the emphasis on the reversal of things in the reign of God. Consequently, forced surrogacy becomes reversed, and those who were forced by oppression into slavery were now envisaged in a new light because the cross symbolized a complete revolution in things.

The cross as a symbol of the reversal of reality needs to be viewed also from the point of view of the eschatological community. From an eschatological community and narrative focus, the cross is an essential dimension of the unfolding story of God. The cross is not salvation; however, it is part of the process that leads to salvation. It is an important episode in the unfolding rule of God. Redemption, as a holistic process, involves the cross as a symbol of reversal, the resurrection and the bestowing of the Holy Spirit to the church. Neither the cross nor the resurrection can be dominant. Rather, it is the holistic work of God that brings about salvation.

The implication of this emphasis on the holistic drama of God's salvation that includes the cross, resurrection, and the coming of the Holy Spirit for the concern of abuse needs special attention. The major concern is how pastoral counselors help counselees in marriage and family life to balance self-love and other-love. The crucial concern is to make sure that one's own validation of self does not come at the expense of another's validation.

This concern for balance has gender implications as well. On the one hand, women who are controlled by the surrogacy view of their role need to be challenged to focus more on self-care and self-focus to bring a healthier balance between self-love and other-love. They need help to see that the cross refers to a reversal of reality where the abused and oppressed will be liberated and validated. On the other hand, men, who find themselves living at the expense of their mates' growth and development and are exploiting surrogacy, need to recognize that the reversal of things in God's plan makes them vulnerable to God's judgment. They also need to develop the other-love dimension to balance their self-love and male privilege. To put these conclusions into more theological language, women, who are controlled by the image of sacrificial surrogacy, need to emphasize the reversal dimension of the cross and the power of the resurrection more than the surrogacy view of the cross and self-sacrifice. Men, however, need to balance self-love and self-focus with self-sacrifice and concern for the growth of others.

The significance of this theological discussion for this chapter is that abuse in marriages and families often comes because of surrogacy and the imbalance of self-love and other love. In the eschatological community view of things, surrogacy is overturned and the balancing of self and other love becomes central to how the people live between the times. Consequently, how pastoral counselors help marital partners and family members to balance self-love and other-love in the pastoral counseling relationship is a central task in marriage and family counseling with African Americans.

For me, abuse is sacrificing the growth of another to secure one's own growth. Therefore, abuse does not have to be physical. However, physical abuse is often the result of attempting to assert one's power over another to assure one's ability to live at the expense of another. Consequently, the defining of abuse covers subjects of rape, incest, and physical abuse along with other issues. More will be said about the nature of violence between African American spouses in the next section.

African American Spouse Violence

Severe violence between African American spouses relates to kicking, biting, hitting with fists, hitting with objects, physical beating, threatening with guns or knives, and the use of guns or knives.[12] A study of severe violence between African American husbands and wives concludes that between 1975 and 1985 severe violence perpetrated toward African American women decreased from 169 per 1,000 persons in 1975 to 64 per 1,000 in 1985.[13] The reasons given for the decline are (1) rise in median income of black males during this period, (2) rise in the age of first marriage, and (3) declining rates of unemployment.[14]

During the same period the study of severe violence of African American women toward African American men increased from 76 per 1,000 in 1975 to 108 per 1,000 in 1985.[15] The explanation for the increase includes (1) self-defense by women, (2) increased consciousness about wife abuse and courage to fight back, (3) feeling less subordinate and more self-love, (4) feeling less dependent on males for economic survival, (5) increase in social class status of females, and (6) increase in families headed by African American women.[16] It was also pointed out that the origin of violence of women toward men includes self-defense, instigation of mutual violence, and sole perpetration of violence.

The major cause of African American male violence toward their spouses was jealousy.[17] Moreover, it was found that shared decision making and egalitarian spousal relationships fostered less violence than the traditional and patriarchal style of spousal relationships. In addition, environmental factors related to how marital partners were raised were significant in the use of

violence. "Violence in the partner's family of origin and its interactional effects with social class and with levels of marital discord explain further how
the variable affects violence in marital relationships."[18]

Sex role socialization in the home environment is also a contributing
factor to violence against women. Finally, it is not clear whether the violence in the female's family of origin or in the male's family of origin was
a significant factor in violence.

With brief discussion of the nature of spousal violence it is time to turn
to a case study.

The Case of Mr. and Mrs. N

Mr. N contacted me because he was frustrated in his marriage. He said
his wife had withdrawn emotionally from him, and this caused him much
pain, anguish, and anger. He said that he and his wife had been married for
about two and a half years, and their relationship was very volatile with his
fits of rage, destroying property, and his leaving for a few days to cool off.
I set an appointment to see him and his wife.

Mr. N was forty-one years of age, and Mrs. N was thirty-one. This is
Mr. N's second marriage, and it is Mrs. N's first marriage. Mr. N has two
boys from his first marriage. Their ages are nine and twelve. Mr. N is in
the health care profession and does considerably well. Mrs. N has begun
her career and is in the housing industry. Mr. N has established himself in
the work world, and Mrs. N has not. She is just beginning and desires to
establish herself in her career before there is any thought of children.

Mr. N's parents are alive. However, they are separated, although they
still have an exclusive relationship. They function as husband and wife although they cannot live together. When they live together, there is verbal
and physical violence, but when they live separately, they live very func-
tionally without abuse or violence. Mr. P also has a younger sister, who has
been married for fifteen years. She has teenage children, and her marriage
is moving in a positive direction after many years of marital difficulty.

Mr. N is emotionally cut off from his family of origin. He only contacts
his mother out of a sense of family obligation. He has very little contact
with his father. He does stay in contact with his sister.

Mrs. N's mother has been divorced several times. Her mother and a
stepfather raised her. Her mother is now single, and Mrs. N remembers
being abused mentally by her stepfather. She is close to her family and has
a sister who lived with her. She values contact with her family of origin and
massages these relationships as much as possible.

She is also very resentful that she gave up her job and moved away from
her relatives in order to be married. She felt that she gave up too much.

Joining

The first session with them involved seeking to join the couple relationship by attending to each spouse's view of their problem. Mrs. N expressed how angry she was because Mr. N seemed to be more involved with his children from his previous marriage. He seemed to be preoccupied with their welfare, and the comfort of his first wife. Mr. N acknowledged that family was very important to him, and that the boys were a dominant concern for him. He expressed frustration that he was not able to handle the pressures from his children and the demands of his wife. He felt that he had sacrificed his relationship with his wife, but he said this was the best he could do under the circumstances. He said no matter what he did nothing seemed to please Mrs. N.

Mrs. N expressed anger that he had not resolved the problem with his children and ex-wife. She felt helpless to do anything about it. However, she constantly tried to get him to resolve the issue once and for all. When she realized that he would not take major steps to handle the situation, she withdrew emotionally and sexually from Mr. N. They had not had sex in over six months. Mrs. N also communicated that if she had known that being married to a divorced man with children was so hard, she would not have married Mr. N. She indicated that they had a whirlwind courtship, and they did not get to see each other in a variety of settings. Rarely were they in settings with Mr. N's children to see what it would be like when married.

From the beginning I had anxiety about the explosive nature of their relationship. I paid particular attention to Mr. N's feelings because I felt his anxiety about what was taking place. I felt that the marital conflict could erupt in a severe or violent way during the session. Consequently, I was always careful to check out to see how Mr. N was feeling about what was going on. This helped in the joining process.

Assessment

The Bicultural Challenge

Mr. N did not seem to be caught up in the demands of being successful by societal standards. He made a very comfortable living in the health profession. He owned his house prior to his second marriage. He had two cars. He paid his alimony and child support. He had established himself in his career and had turned his efforts toward his children and his marriage.

Mrs. N had not established herself in her career. Most of her energy was geared toward making a success of her life. She was seeking success and achievement to the point that Mr. N felt that her work came first. She was upset at times that Mr. N was not as ambitious about his career as she was.

I wondered if Mr. N was supportive of her career efforts. She said that he was very supportive of her career efforts. However, he wished that she was more settled about making more of a contribution on the domestic side of things. He felt that she did not balance the career and home very well.

Neither felt the pressure of race on the job. Mrs. N worked primarily for African Americans, and she was well respected for her talents. She was in demand for her skills. Mr. N was self-employed within the health field and could make as much money as he desired. He had no supervisors or bosses to contend with.

Religion was a major problem. Mrs. N was very traditional about marriage and expected to be the traditional housewife. However, she thought that she could balance home and work very well. She bought into the traditional religious value system on male and female relationships and left her relatives and job to follow her husband as the scriptures recommended. However, there was conflict between her religious views and her desire to be successful in her career and in the home. When the domestic problems dominated, she would withdraw into her work.

Mr. N was not religious at all. He used to be extremely involved with the church, but he became very disaffected by the behavior of his pastor. He calls himself agnostic. While he professes no faith, he has very traditional expectations about male and female relationships although he believes he needs to be supportive of his wife's career goals. Yet he expects her to be able to put the domestic side over her career concerns.

One important issue surfaced in our counseling together—compulsive masculinity. When things were not going well in their marriage, the feelings about compulsive masculinity would surface. One aspect of compulsive masculinity has to do with respect that one receives from another.[19] Sometimes disrespect is interpreted as degrading another's vulnerability and ridiculing this vulnerability. Another potential source of disrespect is the withdrawal of affection through sexual relationships. Often, this is experienced as rejection and abandonment by some males who have been shaped by compulsive masculinity. Mr. N raised all these concerns.

It was not clear to me whether gender norms of beauty affected Mrs. N or not. She never expressed directly any concern about her body or its inadequacy. She seemed confident about her physical attractiveness, and this could have been because she approached the gender norm of wider culture in her skin color and physical appearance.

In summary, the chief conflict in their marriage from the external stressor perspective was the conflicting values related to balancing career and work. Traditional religious values played a significant role in the conflict between them. Moreover, there was a concern for compulsive masculinity as a learned response to external oppression.

Vertical Stressors

Vertical problems were significant for both Mr. and Mrs. N. They inherited patterns from their families of origin that compounded their lives. The most significant patterns for Mr. N had to do with a history of spousal abuse, being assigned adult responsibility as a child, and emotional cutoff from the family of origin.

Mr. N described his relationship with his father as nonexistent. He said that he was always afraid of his father. He said his father was physically abusive toward him, and he felt that his father was very disappointed in him. He also indicated that he saw his mother physically abused and tried to intervene on one occasion when a child. He said his father gave him the severest beating at that time that he had ever had. He interpreted this to mean that his father would kill him if he ever sought to intervene on behalf of his mother. Therefore, Mr. N was beset by feelings of helplessness to do anything about the domestic violence. He kept his feelings bottled up inside himself.

Mr. N also had grown not to like his mother. Because of the domestic strain between his mother and father, his mother turned to Mr. N for help. He said she presented herself as a helpless person, and she depended on him. She confided in him. He was angry because he had to be her parent while his needs for both parents went unattended. He felt orphaned, on the one hand, but like a parent to his parents on the other hand. He felt that he became an expert at caretaking.

Mr. N said that Mrs. N often reminded him of his mother. He said that this would cause him to rage inside. She seemed to be wrapped up in her own feelings like his mother and was not available to him. He felt that he always had to be supportive, and that he felt like he did when he was a child. He didn't think that he could live with Mrs. N having these feelings. He said that he had been unhappy since the marriage began.

Mr. N was cut off from his family of origin. He stayed away from his mother as much as possible to avoid being drawn into the marital difficulties between his parents. His parents were still married, but separated. They, however, saw themselves as husband and wife. When there was conflict, his mother would call him. He hated this. He had very little contact with his father. He also had some contact with his sister, but he thought that this could be improved as well.

Mrs. N reported anger at the fact that her mother had several marriages, and she had several stepfathers. She remembered once not being picked up as a child for one of her mother's weddings. She indicated that this hurt a great deal. She seemed unwilling to explore in any depth this side of her feelings, however. She seemed to want to keep them hidden. There was also some hint at some abuse, but she would not explore any of this. I felt that she had a whole life that she tried to keep hidden from me and her husband that made it difficult to do marital counseling. In one of the private sessions Mr. N felt that he was working very hard to get his personal life together, but that his wife was not putting forth the same effort.

In summary, the family of origin patterns of Mr. and Mrs. N were very involved in their marital problems. Mr. N had a legacy of physical abuse perpetrated against him and his mother by his father. He also was drawn into a relationship with his mother that reversed the parenting roles. Mrs. N also had her needs for nurture and love ignored, and she found it hard to explore these needs in therapy. Apparently, she handled her needs for love and affection by withdrawing into herself and her work. Neither seemed that well differentiated from these problems, and they brought these family patterns into the marriage. Mrs. N brought from her family of origin a pattern of being used to being ignored and left out. Mr. N brought an abusive pattern and a history of not having his needs met from his family of origin. These factors made the marriage very volatile.

Horizontal Stressors

The fact that Mr. and Mrs. N were in two different individual life cycles added to the problem. Moreover, the fact that Mr. N was in his second marriage and Mrs. N was in her first marriage was a major developmental difficulty that they had to face. I think that Mrs. N summed it up quite well when she said they really had not gotten to know each other well prior to the marriage. She felt they had a whirlwind courtship that ignored getting to participate with each other in different settings. Mrs. N said she had no idea how difficult it would be for her to adjust to Mr. N's children and his commitment to them, and she was completely unprepared for this.

Mr. N also felt that he was being asked to make a decision between the marriage or his children. He didn't feel he could make this decision. Therefore, he felt the added pressure of her disappointment in him for not being able to decide between his children or his wife.

Mention has already been made of their different career aspirations. Mr. N felt secure in his career, while Mrs. N was getting herself established. He supported Mrs. N's aspirations, but he definitely wished that she was further along in her career goals than she was.

In summary, each spouse had very little appreciation of the other's individual developmental needs. Their age difference was a major source of stress. They were in the formation stage of their marriage when they were discovering things that could have been discovered during the courtship. In addition, this was the second marriage for Mr. N, and he was less flexible than he could have been if this had been his first marriage. All these developmental factors contributed to cluster stress or multiple levels of stress at the same time. Adding cluster stress to their inherited family of origin patterns made their relationship quite explosive.

Marital Assessment

Many things go into determining whether or not the marital relationship facilitates the growth and development of each spouse. These factors have been enumerated as emotional climate, maintaining the marital relationship through communication and shared activity, marital fusion, major conflicts, type of marital paradigms, triangles, and theological assessment. Several of the factors are explored briefly below.

The climate in the marriage of Mr. and Mrs. N was hot; there was not much safety, and their relationship was turbulent. They had difficulty communicating around significant issues. Only Mr. N would express himself freely, while Mrs. N kept most of her thoughts to herself. There was very little support of one spouse for the other. They had ceased all activity together. Therefore, there was emotional distancing between them. There was conflict over sex and parenting.

It is very difficult to determine what kind of marital paradigm they shared together. It was a combination of closed/traditional and random/individualistic. I think that the underlying model they shared was closed/traditional with careers of both as part of the mix. When there was emotional distancing between them, however, they seemed to be moving toward the random/individualistic model where their individual needs seemed more important than their marital relationship.

Generally, their triangles proved to be benign. That is, they did very little pulling in of others into their relationship. At first, it appeared that Mr. N triangled with the children of his first marriage. But as the story emerged, he seemed to have kept the boundaries between his second marriage and his children clear.

One of the major factors involved in their marital relationship was the level of hostility and violence present. Mr. N would get extremely angry and violent when he felt that Mrs. N had withdrawn affection from him and was shutting him out. He never hit her because he did not want to be like his father. He would leave before things got violent. However, he would destroy property and valuable things in the home as a means to express his rage. This would frighten Mrs. N, but she was not intimidated. Yet she would withdraw into herself.

It was also discovered that Mrs. N had deep-seated anger as well. This anger was present prior to their marital relationship and related to some unresolved issues from her family of origin. This could also be said for Mr. N as well. His father's violence and his mother's manipulation of him were the sources of his anger and rage. However, it was very difficult to explore the sources of Mrs. N's anger.

Theologically, their marital relationship was not very nurturing, nor was the environment suitable for their personal growth. Their emotional reactivity toward each other, and their emotional distancing made it difficult for them to enact the ethic of love. At times they could support the other's growth needs, but this always proved to be very temporary. The resentment that they had toward each other would always enter in and undermine their support growth efforts. In short, their marriage involved a growth-inhibiting environment.

There is also a need to explore briefly how each spouse balanced his or her self-love with other-love in order to complete the theological analysis. Mr. N had an imbalance between self-love and other-love. He felt that he had sacrificed himself as a child caring for his mother. Therefore, he felt that he was entitled to put self-love central and not be concerned about other-love very much. This was the basis of the imbalance with Mr. N.

Mrs. N also had an imbalance between self-love and other-love. As a child she was also expected to sacrifice her self for the sake of others. Gender stereotypes and religious values reinforced this self-sacrifice. When she had to sacrifice too much of herself, she would emotionally withdraw in order to protect herself. However, there were not too many sanctions from others for her to develop self-love. She felt this particularly from Mr. N.

This imbalance between self-love and other-love that both had needed to be dealt with in the pastoral counseling. My concern was to help them bring a balance between these two needs in order for them to grow into their full possibilities as participants in the eschatological community.

Marital Intervention

After joining their marital relationship and clarifying the presenting problem, I introduced to them some goals around which there could be negotiation for the counseling. The primary goal that they saw was the need to give marital counseling a last try to see if it could save their marriage. My input related to the fact that they had emotionally distanced themselves one from the other. Consequently, I said that my first task would be to help each of them explore in depth his or her feelings in the other's presence while the other spouse listened. I indicated that I wanted to model empathy. I also felt that there were some family of origin issues that were unresolved, and I expected to explore some of these issues as well. I also shared that attending to these personal issues could help them to decide whether to stay together or separate. I also indicated that there would be times in the marital counseling where the focus would be directly on their marital relationship.

The basic rationale for addressing the family of origin material was the level of emotional reactivity between them. I felt that the emotional reactivity had to be lessened first before it was possible to deal with the marital relationship itself. This proved true in the case of Mr. N. As he did family of origin work (including making contact with his mother, sister, and father) and explored his feelings, he became clearer about why he behaved so violently. Mrs. N was delighted by the personal discoveries that her husband made, and some improvement in their marital interaction began. However, when Mr. N felt that Mrs. N was not really putting forth any effort to explore her own family of origin issues, he was upset. He eventually decided to terminate counseling as a result and to seek a divorce. He felt that he was not the only one with problems; he felt that the marriage could only survive if both grew.

On several occasions I raised the question of seeing each of them alone. Mrs. N refused to do so feeling that they should stay together. Mr. N did agree, and I saw him twice alone. We worked on how he could reconnect and reenter his family of origin. However, he refused to see me again alone, because he felt that he was the only one working and his wife was not.

This brings up the concern raised earlier about whether African American couples prefer to be seen together rather than separately. Given the problem-solving orientation of many of the couples and families I see, it is logical to think that they could view individual sessions as not related to the presenting problem. Moreover, because of the participatory and interactional orientation of many African Americans, the couple modality may be more preferable. This is important for any therapist to know when working with African American couples, especially.

The Problem of Violence
in African American Marriages

I have learned some things in the case about violence that I think can be further investigated for whether they can be applied to other cases. Although Mr. N had not physically struck Mrs. N, the potential was there, and Mr. N knew it. This potential for violence led Mr. N to seek a divorce rather than risk physical violence.

No one factor was salient in Mr. N's use of violence, for example, when he destroyed property. There were many factors: (1) the shifting back and forth from the closed/traditional paradigm and the random/individualistic model; (2) his loss of religious grounding and his becoming an agnostic were also important in the explosive mix; (3) his family legacy of violence; (4) his feeling he was coerced into caring for his mother as a child were all key factors in the formation of violent responses in him; and (5) compulsive masculinity he developed by participating in African American male culture. However, I think that the major factor in the trigger of violence was the withdrawal of affection from him. This brought into play the compulsive masculinity feelings and legacy of abuse in his family of origin. These five factors led to primitive feelings of being abandoned and rejected which triggered hurt and rage. His customary method of responding to these kinds of feelings was physical.

His personal mythology also figured in the violent response. He equated emotional withdrawal with rejection of self. When this happened negative convictions and beliefs about his self-worth were triggered. Consequently, the feelings of being worthless surfaced, and violence was a way to protect and to defend the self from the feelings of worthlessness. Here personal mythology and the ideology of compulsive masculinity were related.

Mrs. N did not reveal very much about her family of origin, but there were signs that it was abusive and that she could have been abused. There was some indication that she had learned some internalized self-hatred from her family of origin experience. How much this contributed to the explosive nature of their relationship is not known. However, Mr. N felt that something in Mrs. N's past made abusing her easy. He wanted out of the relationship before he turned to violence given his own volatile background.

The intervention strategy with Mr. N as well as with Mrs. N was to relate first to their level of hurt or their tender core. In Mr. N's case this meant attending to his feelings of worthlessness when he felt Mrs. N withdrew from him emotionally. Effort was made to help him understand why he responded with physical violence. He began to understand the family of origin sources of his responses. However, he felt that Mrs. N's own unresolved problems would be such that their relationship would remain explosive if they tried to make a go of their marriage. Consequently, he initiated divorce.

Theologically, violence or the threat of violence destroys the potential for growth and violates the ethic of love. Consequently, divorce is a viable option when the threat of violence remains. The cases of violence where I have been the counselor have usually ended in divorce. I think the reason was that one or both of the spouses realized that the explosive interpersonal dynamics were so volatile that the only solution for them was divorce.

In propositional theology divorce is not permitted except on traditional grounds of adultery. Since violence is so destructive to the personhood of all involved, divorce is a viable alternative. This is consistent with the ethic of love and the norm of growth. I think, however, that a propositional norm for limiting divorce to adultery and/or the use of physical violence needs to be maintained at the macro rational level as a guiding norm to help people at the micro level not to take marriage too lightly.

Intervention and Violence

The pastoral counselor must address violence immediately without hesitation. If there is actual physical violence, the pastoral counselor needs to take the prophetic stance that this is unacceptable and counseling cannot proceed if violence does not stop. Because of the potential for escalating violence of men against women today, it might be important to report any cases of violence to the authorities. This might preclude any pastoral counseling, and this would mean that referrals would have to take place.

As in the case with addictions, I never work with violence unless the violent person agrees to become part of a group for perpetrators of violence. Moreover, it would be good for the wife to get involved with a program for battered wives. There are some realities about violence that need special treatment.

I can work on the personal and family of origin issues with a couple where violence had existed if the violence and the threat of violence have stopped. However, the first order of business for the pastoral counselor is to get the violence and threat of violence stopped immediately. Fourth-party referrals may be the only way to stop the violence so that the therapy can begin.

I did not refer Mr. and Mrs. N to such programs, because there was no physical battering. Moreover, Mr. N realized his potential for violence and faced it head-on. He knew the explosive nature of his past and decided that divorce was the best alternative.

Summary

The primary purpose of this book was to address the problem of growing numbers of African American marriages and families adopting the closed/traditional paradigm represented by some in the Christian church. The aim of the book has been to present an alternative model that also has theological and biblical roots. A model of marriage and family counseling was presented that integrated the theological and the behavioral sciences that addressed how a narrative process model could operate and make marriages and families functional. The ultimate goal of the model, however, was not to improve marriages and families. The ultimate goal of marriage and family pastoral counseling was to enable these marriages and families to be settings where each marital partner and family member could grow into their full possibilities as participants in God's unfolding drama of salvation.

Notes

Chapter 1.
Beyond African American Male Hierarchical Leadership

1. Nancy Boyd-Franklin, *Black Families in Therapy: A Multisystems Approach* (New York: Guilford Press, 1989); Henry Mitchell and Nicholas Lewter, *Soul Theology* (San Francisco: Harper & Row, 1986).

2. See Edward P. Wimberly, "Pastoral Counseling with African American Males," *Urban League Review* 16 (1993): 82–83.

3. These three approaches are modifications of the approaches to doctrine found in the work of George A. Lindbeck, *The Nature of Doctrine: Religion and Theology in a Postliberal Age* (Philadelphia: Westminster Press, 1984), 16–29. The modifications relate to how individual marriages and families formulate their approach to using scripture.

4. Ibid., 32–33.

5. See Edward P. Wimberly, *Using Scripture in Pastoral Counseling* (Nashville: Abingdon Press, 1994).

6. Michael Goldberg, *Theology and Narrative: A Critical Introduction* (Nashville: Abingdon Press, 1981), 35.

7. Ibid., 34.

8. Ibid., 35.

9. Ibid.

10. The view that makes the rule of God or kingdom of God central in the narrative history of the Christian church come from the work of Stanley Hauerwas. See Stanley Hauerwas, *A Community of Character: Toward a Constructive Christian Social Ethic* (Notre Dame, Ind.: University of Notre Dame Press, 1981), 37. I am also indebted to H. Richard Niebuhr, *The Meaning of Revelation* (New York: Macmillan Co., 1941), 32–66 for his understanding of revelation in history.

11. Niebuhr, *The Meaning of Revelation*, 59–66.

12. Ibid., 61.

13. See Anne Streaty Wimberly and Edward P. Wimberly, *The Language of Hospitality: Intercultural Relations in the Household of God* (Nashville: Cokesbury), 42–47.

14. This method is used by William B. Oglesby in *Biblical Themes in Pastoral Care* (Nashville: Abingdon Press, 1980), 33.

15. Charles S. Finch, *Echoes of the Old Darkland: Themes from the African Eden* (Atlanta: Khenti, 1991).

16. See E. P. Wimberly, "Pastoral Counseling with African American Males," 79.

17. Finch, *Echoes of the Old Darkland*, xiii.

Chapter 2.
Male and Female, God Created Them to Be Whole

1. See James H. Cone, *My Soul Looks Back* (Nashville: Abingdon Press, 1986); Mitchell and Lewter, *Soul Theology.*

2. Alfred B. Pasteur and Ivory L. Toldson, *Roots of Soul: The Psychology of Black Expressiveness* (Garden City, N.Y.: Doubleday & Co., Anchor Books, 1982).

3. Linda H. Hollies, ed., *Womanist Care: How to Tend the Souls of Women* (Joliet, Ill.: Woman to Woman Ministries, 1991).

4. Anne Streaty Wimberly, *Soul Stories: African American Christian Education* (Nashville: Abingdon Press, 1995).

5. Mitchell and Lewter, *Soul Theology*, ix–x.

6. Ibid., 5.

7. Ibid.

8. Ibid.

9. Ibid., 6.

10. Ibid., 8.

11. Ibid., 8–9.

12. Edward P. Wimberly, *Pastoral Counseling and Spiritual Values: A Black Point of View* (Nashville: Abingdon Press, 1982), 42–43.

13. For a discussion of the Platonic and Gnostic view of human beings, see A. W. Richard Sipe, "Sexual Aspects of the Human Condition," in *Changing Views of the Human Condition*, ed. Paul W. Pruyser (Macon, Ga.: Mercer University Press, 1987), 81–100.

14. *Dictionary of Pastoral Care and Counseling* (Nashville: Abingdon Press, 1990), 1201–1202. For a discussion of how some of the biblical material in the New Testament was a reaction to a mind and body dualism, see Khiok-Khng Yeo, "Rhetorical Interaction I Corinthians 8 and 10: Potential Implications for a Chinese, Cross-Cultural Hermeneutic" (Ph.D. diss., Northwestern University, 1993), 198–215.

15. *Dictionary of Pastoral Care and Counseling*, 1202.

16. Alice Walker, *The Third Life of Grange Copeland* (New York: Pocket Books, 1988), 345.

17. For a discussion of the soul as center of the person's life, see Edward P. Wimberly and Anne Streaty Wimberly, *Liberation and Human Wholeness: The Conversion Experiences of Black People in Slavery and Freedom* (Nashville: Abingdon Press, 1986), 99–100.

18. Ibid.

19. Riggins R. Earl Jr. explores in depth how the slaves developed an embodied soul. See his *Dark Symbols, Obscure Signs: God, Self and Community in the Slave Mind* (Maryknoll, N.Y.: Orbis Books, 1993), 4–7.

20. Mitchell and Lewter, *Soul Theology*, 113.

21. See Phyllis Bird, "Male and Female He Created Them," *Harvard Theological Review* 74 (April 1981): 129–59.

22. Phyllis Trible, *God and the Rhetoric of Sexuality* (Philadelphia: Fortress Press, 1978), 73.

23. Ibid., 128.

24. Robert Jewett, *Paul the Apostle to America: Cultural Trends and Pauline Scholarship* (Louisville, Ky.: Westminster John Knox, 1994), 45–58.

25. Elisabeth Schüssler Fiorenza, *In Memory of Her: A Feminist Theological Reconstruction of Christian Origins* (New York: Crossroad, 1992), 235–36.

26. Mitchell and Lewter, *Soul Theology*, 127.

27. Most of the references used here are found in two sources that my wife and I have written: Anne Streaty Wimberly and Edward Powell Wimberly, *One Household and One Hope: Building Ethnic Minority Clergy Family Support Networks* (Nashville: General Board of Higher Education and Ministry, United Methodist Church, 1988), and Wimberly and Wimberly, *Language of Hospitality.*

28. J. Deotis Roberts, *Liberation and Reconciliation: A Black Theology* (Philadelphia: Westminster Press, 1971), 66.

29. This paragraph reflects conclusions that are found in Wimberly and Wimberly, *One Household and One Hope*, 9.

30. Wimberly and Wimberly, *Language of Hospitality*, 74.

31. Roberts, *Liberation and Reconciliation*, 68.

32. Ibid., 67.

33. Robert Jewett, "Tenement Churches and Pauline Love Feasts," *Quarterly Review*, May 1994, 46–50.

34. Ibid., 55.

Chapter 3.
The Context of African American Families

1. The following articles in journals, chapters in books, and books express the importance of putting African Americans in the cultural context in counseling and psychotherapy: Lily D. McNair, "African American Women in Therapy: An Afrocentric and Feminist Synthesis," *Women in Therapy* 12 (1992): 5–19; Anderson J. Franklin, "Therapy with African American Men," *Families in Society* 73 (June 1992): 350–55; Stephen A. McLeod-Bryant, "Racism and Psychotherapy," *American Journal of Psychiatry* 150 (July 1993): 1128–29; Howard C. Stevenson and Gary Renard, "Trusting Ole' Wise Owls: Therapeutic Use of Cultural Strengths in African American Families," *Professional Psychology Research in Practice* 24 (November 1993): 433–42; Beverly Greene, "Psychotherapy with African-American Women: Integrating Feminist and Psychodynamic Models," *Journal of Training and Practice in Professional Psychology* 7 (Spring 1993): 49–66; Beth S. Richie, "Coping with Work: Interventions with African-American Women," *Women in Therapy* 12 (1992): 97–111; Ronnie Priest, "Racism and Prejudice as Negative Impacts on African American Clients in Therapy," *Journal of Counseling and Development* 70 (September–October 1991): 213–15; Anderson J. Franklin, "An Integrative Approach to Psychotherapy with Black/African Americans: The Relevance of Race and Culture," in *Comprehensive Handbook of Psychotherapy Integration*, ed. George Stricker and Jerold R. Gold (New York: Plenum Press, 1993), 465–79; Arthur C. Jones, "African Americans: A Conceptual Guide for Use in Psychotherapy," in *Black Psychology*, ed. Reginald L. Jones (Berkeley, Calif.: Cobb

& Henry, 1991), 577–89; A. Kathleen Burlew et al., eds., *African American Psychology: Theory, Research, and Practice* (Newbury Park, Calif.: Sage Publications, 1992).

2. W.E.B. Du Bois, *The Souls of Black Folk* (Chicago: A. C. McClurg & Co. 1903; reprint, Greenwich, Conn.: Fawcett, 1961), 16.

3. Andrew Billingsley, *Climbing Jacob's Ladder: The Enduring Legacy of African-American Families* (New York: Simon & Schuster, 1992), 224.

4. Ibid., 20.

5. Wimberly and Wimberly, *Language of Hospitality*, 77.

6. Lena Wright Myers, "Reflections: Some Empirical Comments on Early Socialization of African American Men," *Bulletin: Morehouse Research Institute* 4 (1993): 1–3.

7. Renita J. Weems, *I Asked for Intimacy: Stories of Blessings, Betrayals, and Birthings* (San Diego: LuraMedia, 1993), 47.

8. Internalized racism also involves African Americans internalizing white racist stereotypes about them. To the extent that this is done, internalized racism impacts marital satisfaction. There was some evidence that both spouses had internalized some racial stereotypes. For a discussion of internalized racism and marital satisfaction see Jerome Taylor, "Relationship Between Internalized Racism and Marital Satisfaction," in *African American Psychology: Theory, Research, and Practice*, ed. A. Kathleen Burlew et al. (Newbury Park, Calif.: Sage Publications, 1992): 127–34.

9. Katie G. Cannon, *Black Womanist Ethics* (Atlanta: Scholars Press, 1988), 89.

10. Ibid., 90.

11. Myers, "Reflections," 3.

12. See C. Eric Lincoln and Lawrence H. Mamiya, *The Black Church in the African American Experience* (Durham, N.C.: Duke University Press, 1990), 3.

13. Ibid., 4–5.

14. Delores P. Aldridge, *Focusing: Black Male-Female Relationships* (Chicago: Third World Press, 1991), 21.

15. Ibid., 22.

16. Ibid.

17. E. P. Wimberly, "Pastoral Counseling with African American Males," 79.

18. Delores S. Williams, *Sisters in the Wilderness: The Challenge of Womanist God-Talk* (Maryknoll, N.Y.: Orbis Books, 1993), 71–72.

19. Ibid., 72.

20. Weems, *I Asked for Intimacy*, 62.

21. Ibid., 64.

22. Ibid., 66.

23. E. P. Wimberly, "Pastoral Counseling with African American Males," 79.

24. Clarence Walker, *Biblical Counseling with African-Americans: Taking a Ride in the Ethiopian's Chariot* (Grand Rapids: Zondervan Publishing House, 1992), 44.

25. Ibid., 45.

Chapter 4.
A Transgenerational View

1. Betty Carter and Monica McGoldrick, "Overview, The Changing Family Life Cycle: A Framework for Family Therapy," in *The Changing Family Life Cycle*, ed. Betty Carter and Monica McGoldrick (Boston: Allyn & Bacon, 1989), 8–9.

2. Michael Nichols, *Family Therapy: Concepts and Methods* (New York: Gardner Press, 1984), 587.

3. Carter and McGoldrick, "Overview," 9.

4. Boyd-Franklin, *Black Families in Therapy*, 76–77.

5. See ibid. and Paulette Moore Hines, "The Family Life Cycle of Poor Black Families," in *Changing Family Life Cycle*, Carter and McGoldrick, 525.

6. Boyd-Franklin, *Black Families in Therapy*, 77.

7. Ibid., 70.

8. See Cannon, *Black Womanist Ethics*.

9. Murray Bowen, *Family Therapy in Clinical Practice* (New York: Jason Aronson, 1978), 382.

10. Boyd-Franklin, *Black Families in Therapy*, 219–20.

11. Ibid., 126–28.

12. Ibid., 126.

13. Ibid.

14. Michael E. Kerr and Murray Bowen, *Family Evaluation* (New York: W. W. Norton & Co., 1988), 224–25.

15. Boyd-Franklin, *Black Families in Therapy*, 127.

16. Ibid., 233.

17. Kerr and Bowen, *Family Evaluation*, 225.

18. Delores P. Aldridge, *Black Male-Female Relationships: A Resource Book of Selected Materials* (Dubuque, Iowa: Kendall/Hunt Publishing Co., 1989), and *Focusing: Black Male-Female Relationships*.

19. Aldridge, *Focusing*, 19–27.

20. Ibid., 21.

21. Ibid., 22.

22. Ibid., 23.

23. Aldridge, *Black Male-Female Relationships*, 6.

24. Ibid., 7.

25. Ibid.

26. Ibid., 8–9.

27. Ibid., 12.

28. See Wimberly and Wimberly, *Language of Hospitality*, 38.

29. Carolyn McCrary, "Interdependency as a Norm: An Interdisciplinary Model of Pastoral Counseling" (S.T.D. diss., Interdenominational Theological Center, 1989).

30. E. P. Wimberly, "Pastoral Counseling with African American Males," 77.

31. Boyd-Franklin, *Black Families in Therapy*, 191.

32. Ibid.

33. Ibid., 191–92.

34. Ibid.
35. Ibid., 193.
36. Ibid., 201.
37. Ibid., 202.
38. William C. Nichols and Craig A. Everett, *Systemic Family Therapy: An Integrative Approach* (New York: Guilford Press, 1986), 185–86.

Chapter 5.
The Horizontal Context: The Life Cycle

1. For a discussion of the significance of Erik Erikson and Daniel Levinson for African Americans, see Edward P. Wimberly, "A Conceptual Model of Pastoral Care for the Black Church Utilizing Systems and Crisis Theories" (Ph.D. diss., Boston University Graduate School, 1975), 64–85; Reginald L. Jones, ed., *Black Adult Development and Aging* (Berkeley, Calif.: Cobb & Henry, 1989); Arthur C. Jones, "Psychological Functioning in African-American Adults: Some Elaborations on a Model, with Clinical Implications," in ibid., 297–307; Janice E. Ruffin, "Stages of Adult Development in Black, Professional Women," in ibid., 31–61; Winston E. Gooden, "Development of Black Men in Early Adulthood," in ibid., 63–89.

2. Gooden talks about the limitations of Levinson's theories in "Development of Black Men in Early Adulthood," 88.

3. See Wade W. Nobles, "African Philosophy: Foundations for Black Psychology," in *Black Psychology*, ed. Reginald L. Jones (New York: Harper & Row, 1980), 23–36.

4. Ibid., 33.

5. Ibid., 27.

6. Gooden, "Development of Black Men in Early Adulthood," 88.

7. Romney Moseley, *Becoming a Self Before God: Critical Transformations* (Nashville: Abingdon Press, 1991), 70.

8. See E. P. Wimberly, "Pastoral Counseling with African American Males," 77–84.

9. Billingsley, *Climbing Jacob's Ladder*, 328.

10. Algea O. Harrison, "Black Working Women: Introduction to a Life Span Perspective," in *Black Adult Development and Aging*, ed. Reginald Jones, 91–113.

11. See A. C. Jones, "Psychological Functioning in African-American Adults," 301–2.

12. Ibid., 560.

13. See Billingsley, *Climbing Jacob's Ladder*, 332; and Dennis A. Bagarozzi, "Family Therapy and the Black Middle Class: A Neglected Area of Study," *Journal of Marital and Family Therapy*, April 1980, 159–66.

14. Billingsley, *Climbing Jacob's Ladder*, 332–33.

15. This material is drawn from Hines, "Family Life Cycle of Poor Black Families," 513–44.

16. Ibid., 515.

17. Ibid., 516.

18. Ibid., 517.
19. William C. Nichols and Craig A. Everett have helped me to understand the multilevel approach to the life cycle in *Systemic Family Therapy*, 142–75.
20. Ibid., 149.
21. Dennis Bagarozzi and Stephen Anderson, *Personal, Marital, and Family Myths* (New York: W. W. Norton & Co., 1989), 15–16.
22. William C. Nichols, *Marital Therapy: An Integrative Approach* (New York: Guilford Press, 1988), 20–21. The terms of care, commitment, communication, conflict, and compromise are defined in this work.
23. Bagarozzi and Anderson, *Personal, Marital, and Family Myths*, 17–18.
24. Ibid., 77.
25. Ibid., 78.
26. Ibid.
27. Ibid., 79.
28. Nichols and Everett, *Systemic Family Therapy*, 160–66.
29. Ibid.
30. Billingsley, *Climbing Jacob's Ladder*, 332.
31. Nichols and Everett, *Systemic Family Therapy*, 167–70.
32. Nydia Garcia Preto, "Transformation of the Family System in Adolescence," in *Changing Family Life Cycle*, Carter and McGoldrick, 255–83.
33. Nichols, "Family System Tasks."
34. Ibid.

Chapter 6.
A Model of Joining, Assessment, and Intervention

1. Boyd-Franklin, *Black Families in Therapy*, 96.
2. Ibid., 97.
3. Ibid.
4. Thomas J. Pugh, "Attitudes of Black Women and Men Toward Using Community Services," *Journal of Religion and Health*, July 1971, 256–77. See also Boyd-Franklin, *Black Families in Therapy*, 19.
5. Boyd-Franklin, *Black Families in Therapy*, 19.
6. Boston interpersonalism refers to the work of Paul Johnson at Boston University School of Theology. See Paul Johnson, *Psychology of Pastoral Care: The Pastoral Ministry in Theory and Practice* (Nashville: Abingdon Press, 1953), 8, 27–30.
7. Ivan Boszormenyi-Nagy, "Contextual Therapy: Therapeutic Leverage in Mobilizing Trust," in *Family Therapy: Major Contributions*, ed. R. J. Green and J. L. Framo (New York: International Universities Press, 1981), 404.
8. Paulette Moore Hines, "Black Families," in *Ethnicity and Family Therapy*, ed. Monica McGoldrick, John K. Pearce, and Joseph Giordano (New York: Guilford Press, 1982), 102.
9. Ibid.
10. Ibid.
11. See Jay Haley, *Problem Solving Therapy* (San Francisco: Jossey-Bass, 1976).

12. Ibid., 1.

13. John Patton, *Pastoral Care in Context: An Introduction to Pastoral Care* (Louisville, Ky.: Westminster/John Knox Press, 1993), 40.

14. William Oliver, *The Violent Social World of Black Men* (New York: Lexington Books, 1994), 12.

15. Ibid.

16. This point is made very clear by Anderson J. Franklin in "Therapy with African American Men," *Families in Society* 73 (June 1992): 351. Franklin points out that African American males are not likely to share personal vulnerabilities, to trust therapists, or to give themselves over to the therapeutic process because of problems related to racism and images of what it means to be a man.

17. For a discussion of the internalization of racism of African American women, see Cheryl Townsend Gilkes, "The 'Loves' and 'Troubles' of African-American Women's Bodies: The Womanist Challenge to Cultural Humiliation and Community Ambivalence," in *A Troubling in My Soul: Womanist Perspectives on Evil & Suffering*, ed. Emilie M. Townes (Maryknoll, N.Y.: Orbis Books, 1993), 240–41; Weems, *I Asked for Intimacy*, 62–63.

18. Boyd-Franklin, *Black Families in Therapy*, 142.

19. Ibid., 143.

20. The questions for this section are drawn largely from Philip J. Guerin et al., *The Evaluation and Treatment of Marital Conflict: A Four-Stage Approach* (New York: Basic Books, 1987), 33–60.

21. Michael D. Nugent and Larry L. Constantine, "Marital Paradigms," *Journal of Marital and Family Therapy* 14, no. 4 (1988): 351.

22. Guerin et al. *Evaluation and Treatment of Marital Conflict*, 62–82.

23. Boyd-Franklin, *Black Families in Therapy*, 122–28.

24. Ibid., 122–23.

25. Ibid., 123.

26. Ibid., 127.

27. Ibid.

28. The emphasis on phases comes from Nichols and Everett, *Systemic Family Therapy*, 245–56.

Chapter 7.
Sexual Dysfunction in Marriage

1. For an in-depth discussion of African American sexuality, see Claire Sterk-Elifson, "Sexuality among African-American Women," in *Sexuality Across the Life Course*, ed. Alice S. Rossi (Chicago: University of Chicago Press, 1994), 99–126; and Benjamin P. Bowser, "African-American Male Sexuality through the Early Life Course," in ibid., 127–50.

2. The observations made about sex here come from comments made by female counselees and workshop participants whom I have encountered over the years.

3. See Aldridge, *Black Male-Female Relationships*, 11. Aldridge talks about how black males and females cannot afford to reduce themselves to defining themselves in exclusively sexual or physical terms. This relates back to slavery.

4. Oliver, *Violent Social World of Black Men*, 12.

5. Salvador Minuchin et al., *Families of the Slums: An Exploration of Their Structure and Treatment* (New York: Basic Books, 1967), 219. Although Minuchin is talking about characteristics of the population of poor people, he does include African Americans in his study.

Chapter 8.
Marital Therapy and an Extramarital Affair

1. See William Nichols, "Ambivalence," lecture given as part of the course entitled Evaluation and Treatment of Marital Therapy, Smyrna, Ga., February 8, 1993.

2. Ibid.

3. See Bagarozzi and Anderson, *Personal, Marital and Family Myths*, 17.

4. Gilkes, "The 'Loves' and 'Troubles' of African-American Women's Bodies," 234.

5. Ibid.

6. This analysis is based on the work of William Nichols in his *Marital Therapy*, 3–38.

7. See Michael D. Nugent and Larry L. Constantine, "Marital Paradigms: Compatibility, Treatment, and Outcome in Marital Therapy," *Journal of Marital and Family Therapy* 14 (1988): 353.

8. Daniel J. Levinson, *The Seasons of a Man's Life* (New York: Ballantine Books, 1978), 213–21.

9. This analysis is based on the work of Philip J. Guerin et al. in *Evaluation and Treatment of Marital Conflict*, 33–60.

10. Ibid., 61–119.

11. Ibid., 123.

Chapter 9.
Abuse and Pastoral Counseling

1. Gilkes, "The 'Loves' and 'Troubles' of African-American Women's Bodies," 240.

2. Ibid., 240–41.

3. bell hooks and Cornel West, *Breaking Bread: Insurgent Black Intellectual Life* (Boston: South End Press, 1991), 115.

4. Williams, *Sisters in the Wilderness*, 162.

5. Ibid., 164.

6. Ibid.

7. Ibid., 166.

8. Jacquelyn Grant, "Womanist Jesus and the Mutual Struggle for Liberation," in *Recovery of Black Presence: An Interdisciplinary Exploration*, ed. Randall C. Bailey and Jacquelyn Grant (Nashville: Abingdon Press, 1995), 138.

9. Williams, *Sisters in the Wilderness*, 164.

10. See Edward P. Wimberly, *Adult Bible Studies: Good News for All* (Nashville: Cokesbury), Winter 1992–93, 54–56.

11. Ibid., 56–57.

12. See Robert L. Hampton, Richard J. Gelles, and John Harrop, "Is Violence in Black Families Increasing? A Comparison of 1975 and 1985 National Rates," in *Black Family Violence: Current Research and Theory*, ed. Robert L. Hampton (Lexington, Mass.: Lexington Books, 1991), 3–18.

13. Ibid., 8.

14. Ibid., 14–16.

15. Ibid., 8.

16. Ibid., 15.

17. Lettie L. Lockhart, "Spousal Violence: A Cross Racial Perspective," in *Black Family Violence*, 85–101.

18. Ibid., 100.

19. Oliver, *Violent Social World of Black Men*, 93.

Index